Grant Writing for Educators

Practical Strategies for Teachers, Administrators, and Staff

Beverly A. Browning, MPA, DBA

formerly national educational service

Cover art and design by Grannan Graphic Design, Ltd.

Text design by T.G. Design Group

Printed in the United States of America

ISBN: 1-932127-30-5

Dedication

To my lifetime friend, buddy, and husband, John, who graciously and willingly left his job, friends, and the "paradise-like" Arizona desert to help me in my grant writing consulting business, I cherish you for the many sustaining gifts of love. Your willingness to pack up and move to the mountains of Arkansas means more than you will ever know.

To my dynamic daughter, Lara, whose ever-present dry humor and optimistic attitude inspire me in every area of my life, I offer you this public acknowledgement. Even across the miles, I can hear your voice and see your face every time I have to make a difficult decision. Your gift for repairing fractured families is a testimony of your greatness. To my son-in-law, Charles, who brings balance and wisdom to our zany family, a wish for many future blessings.

To my dear cat, Leggs, I wish you many more cat years in gratitude for your unconditional love for this weary and often cranky grant writer and educator. Surely, there will be a velvet purple cushion for you in the great beyond.

Acknowledgments

First, I wish to thank Jeff Jones, President of Solution Tree (formerly National Educational Service). He motivated me to turn my vision of a practical working guide for educators, administrators, and staff into a real book. Second, I want to thank Suzanne Kraszewski, the Director of Publications. It took me nearly 2 years to formulate a response to her e-mail offer to join the Solution Tree family. Thanks, Suzanne, for not looking for another grant writer to deliver this book. Third, I want to acknowledge all of the Solution Tree staff who worked behind the scenes, especially Larry Ligget, Senior Editor, to further edit and polish this publication. Finally, I wish to thank my proofreader and editor of many years, Doris Maxfield, owner of Max's Word Services in Linden, Michigan. Doris has been my friend and devil's advocate for over a decade. She has never failed me, and most importantly, her impeccable skills have allowed me to focus on the creative parts of writing—not the grammatical. This guide is my thirteenth publication, and by far the easiest. Thanks!

Table of Contents

Becoming a Successful Grant Writer

"How can I teach with no materials or supplies?"

"If I only knew how to write grants and get award money, I could help change things around here."

"Why do others get grant awards and I don't?"

THE PROSPECT OF RESEARCHING a grant and writing the application can be intimidating, especially for busy educators who have much on their plates with the everyday rigors of their jobs. Your interest in reading this book shows you likely have the initiative to become the most successful grant writer in the history of your school; you just need to learn how. It is true that grant awards are not that easy to get and you cannot expect to receive one just because you asked for it, but for educators, administrators, and staff members who take time to investigate three key questions, the odds for writing a successful grant skyrocket. Before putting their fingertips to the keyboard, they know the answers to the following important questions. After reading this book, you will know the answers, too.

1. *Where is the money?* You will learn where to find grant opportunities and how to keep track of them.

2. *What format does a funding agency want to see?* You will be guided in writing winning grant proposals to corporations and foundations.

3. *Exactly what do I have to write in order to receive high review points and win grant awards?* You will understand the ins and outs of applying for a government grant—monies funneled through your state's department of education or the U.S. Department of Education.

Today, most large school districts have dedicated grant writers or full-fledged development offices that churn out corporate requests, foundation proposals, state education agency grant applications, and federal grant applications. Smaller school districts, charter schools, and even individual schools usually do not have the advantage of a dedicated grant writer. Instead, a hurried administrator or a frazzled teacher takes on the task of grant writing, often willingly but unprepared. When their efforts are denied funding, the momentum is filed in the bottom drawer along with a copy of the failed grant application or proposal. But there really is no reason to let rejection letters stop your school from applying for grants again.

A small group of teachers—or even one teacher—can have tremendous success at the grant writing game. It takes leadership, and every school building has these leaders. They are:

- Self-starters (they work on their own initiative)

- Visionaries (they see the big picture)

- Change agents (they make things happen)

- Strategic thinkers (they plan and coordinate)

- Committed individuals (they remain focused)

It is your moment in time to be a leader at writing and acquiring grants for your school or district. This book gives you a tremendous boost—the chapters are filled with expertise and encouragement and are written with the concerns of every educator who has asked, "How can we do this?"

Sharpen your pencils, blow out the dust in your computer mouse, and get ready to combine your writing and computer technology skills with the grant seeking and grant writing tips and knowledge offered in this book.

Chapter 1

Getting Your Share Means Playing an Aggressive Game

GETTING YOUR SHARE OF GRANT MONIES requires winning at the grant game. Why do I call grant seeking a game? Because it is a competitive endeavor requiring skills, strategy, persistence, practice, and the desire to come out on top. Some schools win the grant game, while others lose. The winners take the game seriously, and they take a serious portion of the grants doled out by the U.S. Department of Education and other grant makers. The Department currently (2005) administers a budget of about $63 billion per year and operates programs touching on every area and level of education. The Department's elementary and secondary programs annually serve approximately 14,000 school districts and nearly 54 million students attending more than 93,000 public schools and 27,000 private schools. Department programs also provide grant, loan, and work-study assistance to more than 9.5 million postsecondary students (U.S. Department of Education Web site: http://www.ed.gov/about/overview/budget/ index.html).

In this chapter you will learn where the money comes from: what foundation and corporate grants are and how state and federal governments distribute grants. You will also be given pointers on how to catch up with and join the aggressors in the grant game. If your school needs more money, this book will provide you with valuable information you can use and share with administrators and colleagues.

WHERE DOES THE MONEY COME FROM?

Government Grants

Despite the perception that the federal government is responsible for the bulk of educational spending in America, primary responsibility rests at the state and local levels. In fact, although Congress has increased the president's budget for education every year except one since the early 1990s, the federal government still contributes only 7% of all spending on education. Why? The bulk of the federal allocations for education are monies that are passed down to State Education Agencies (SEAs) for grantmaking purposes.

This money from Washington, D.C., trickles down to each state education agency (commonly called department of education by the individual states). You can locate the address and contact information for your state agency at the U.S. Department of Education Web site: http://wdcrobcolp01.ed.gov/Programs/ EROD/. Click on "Organization By Type," and scroll down to "State Education Agency," click, and the state agencies are listed in alphabetical order.

Once the money arrives in your state, the state education agency retains a portion for program administration costs and places the rest into an allocation fund. States can make two types of allocations to public school districts and charter schools: formula grants and competitive grants. Formula grants take a big chunk from the allocation fund, and are distributed to schools based on their makeup. Any monies left over in the allocation fund are divided into multiple competitive grant applications aimed at improving preschool programs, technology infrastructure, professional development, and a host of other areas.

Dark clouds are looming for states and localities struggling to provide quality education to children. Stateline.org (www.stateline.org/stateline) recently reported that declining tax revenues, exploding school enrollments, and state budget cuts are combining to put increased state spending on education at risk for everything from new buildings and teacher salary hikes to expanded preschool programs.

The competition for money is stiff and although your school's need is great, it must compete against every other public school and charter school in your state. Further, even though the federal government is constantly increasing allocations, there will never be enough money trickling down for your state to award one grant in every county or parish. That is why you must be aggressive in the grant game.

Foundation and Corporate Grants

Foundations and corporations also have money to dole out to causes they deem worthy. These private or not-for-profit organizations have a certain amount of funds earmarked for philanthropy. Your school's area of need could be a perfect match for a corporation's area of interest, and foundations award billions of dollars annually for education programs.

If your funding needs are less than $10,000, route your request to a corporation. Many corporations set aside a percentage of their annual profits for philanthropic initiatives in the communities where they operate. Look around your town and ask yourself, "Who is conducting business?" Talk to your business manager or comptroller to get a list of school or university vendors. Even in dire financial times, larger companies will have reserves set aside for social responsibility.

If your funding needs are greater than $10,000, then you will need to do your homework to identify small- to medium-sized foundations. These grantmakers are typically nonprofit in nature and will have an IRS 501(c)(3) status. This means they can raise funds through solicitation to individuals and larger foundations as well as regrant funds received to fulfill grant proposal requests that meet their funding interests and guidelines.

CHARACTERISTICS OF GRANT WINNING SCHOOLS

What separates the winning schools from the losing schools in the grant game? Winning schools might have full-time grant writers and supporting staff working hard to look for and write grant applications and proposals; however, they might also send teachers and administrators for grant writing training, and then collect a return on the investment by allocating work time to form grant writing teams. Winning schools subscribe to online funding directories, alerts, and newsletters and check them on a daily basis so they know where there is a grant funding opportunity, when the proposal or application is due, and the average amount of the grant award. Winning schools identify needs and seek external funding support to implement research-driven solutions. In other words, grant winning schools work aggressively to keep on top of the grant game, and they continually apply for foundation, corporate, state, and federal grant opportunities.

Is your school a winner at the grant game? If you feel your school is unsuccessful, then it is time for you to learn the grant seeking and grant writing process. Say to yourself, "Enough of this wishful thinking. I'll write the grant applications for the computers, supplies, electronic white boards, and other things that my classroom and school need."

LESSONS LEARNED

Years ago, I lived in a small midwestern town that at one time had been an economically thriving community with 58 schools and widespread district administrative offices. The district had been the recipient of the nation's first foundation grant for after-school enrichment programs. The administration had been so confident that the fiscal security and future growth of the district was cast in stone that they retired their grant writer.

Several years passed and the town's largest employer closed three of its major facilities. Among the workers laid off indefinitely were the parents of school-age children. Families lost their homes and were forced to move elsewhere to seek minimum-wage or service-level employment openings. As the community population and economy diminished, the school corporation lost much of its funding. In panic, the school administrators finally appealed to local foundations and other private sources for major financial assistance. But it was too late; nothing could save the school district from the serious dilemma it faced. Today, 30 schools have been closed. The teachers that remain are counting the days until retirement, and administrators are hoping to stockpile paychecks before they are laid off.

The lesson I learned from observing this situation is that schools that always operate in crisis management style—acting on the moment and failing to look out for tomorrow—do not win. I cannot stress enough how important it is for you to start the ball rolling when it comes to locating grant funding opportunities. Get your administrators to allocate work time to form a team and go after these highly sought after monies. Important action steps for getting started appear below.

ACTION STEPS

Form the team. Search out other teachers and parent/ community volunteers who have an interest in grant writing. Form a small building-level team of 10 or fewer volunteers.

Train the team. Get administration approval and support for team members to attend grant writing training workshops. Some presenters, including this author, deliver customized grant writing workshops for teachers and administrators throughout North America. Many online education vendors such as Education To Go (www.educationtogo.com) offer basic and advanced grant writing classes. I recommend the following courses for educators: A to Z Grantwriting, Get Grants!, Writing Effective Grant Proposals, and Advanced Proposal Writing (taught by Bev Browning).

Feed the team grant funding information. Do a quick survey of all teachers in your building to find out who subscribes to a funding alert. Ask those who receive alerts—free and subscription-based—to forward and share them with others. Also, consider subscribing to free alerts for yourself. (See page 96, Waiting for the E-Mail Alert.)

Chapter 2

Identifying School Projects and Finding Award Money

BECOMING A GRANT SEARCHING DETECTIVE makes you the de facto captain of your district's grant game team. A good grant detective collects a list of colleagues' needs and/or his or her own needs and identifies potential funding opportunities for the school. The "gumshoe" is always alert to notice trends and shifts in funding priorities. The economy and political agendas affect what types of grant programs are available. Some programs have been around for decades but others come and go as quickly as a year after they are introduced. You will need to know what types of programs are currently being funded and be ready to adapt your project goals and objectives, if necessary, so they conform to funding priorities.

IDENTIFY NEEDS

In order to determine your grant funding needs, you must first identify your own needs, the needs of your colleagues, and finally, your district's needs. You can do this quickly by sending out an e-mail asking for a list of needed supplies, equipment, materials, and programs. A form will not be necessary; using e-mail will reduce your response and information review time. Once you have a stack of replies, sort them based on common response areas (categories): mathematics, reading, social studies, arts, consumer science, technology, physical fitness, and so forth. The largest department or academic area will not necessarily always have the largest stack of grant funding needs. Often the largest academic area is quite proficient at getting competitive grants and may even have a larger earmarking of Title 1 (entitlement) funds. Often the smallest department will have the greatest grant funding needs because they are overlooked as "essential" by administration; they have no cadre of educators looking for funding opportunities and writing grant proposals. Sometimes, numbers can outweigh need. Handle inequities by addressing each of the academic departments over a given period of time. For example: English Language Arts (ELA) may have the greatest need due to the No Child Left Behind mandates. However, only write a grant project for ELA once or twice per school year. ELA will have to cycle in and out of your priorities so that you can address other department's needs—treating each area equally. Technology needs will always have the largest cost factor because technology usually requires new physical infrastructure work, tons of new equipment, more professional development training, and is often outdated soon after installation.

SEARCH FOR COMPATIBLE FUNDING PARTNERS

A fundamental rule of the grant game is to approach only those funders interested in awarding grants in the same area as your need. Start your search for a compatible funding partner by first finding funders that make grants in the area of your project. Here is a list of the project areas that are of interest to grant funders:

- Building or renovation funds (for nothing major)

- Conferences and seminars (for educational purposes, such as learning new mathematics pedagogy or reviewing a new character education curriculum)

- Consultation services (for experts providing staff development workshops, including those on grant writing)

- Curriculum development (for all framework areas)

- Challenge or matching funds (for leveraging monies to win additional grant awards)

- Equipment (for technology and other tools)

- Program development (for creating new or expanded programs)

- Program evaluation (for tracking short- and long-term program impact)

- Publications (for distributing information to constituents such as the school newspaper, bulletins for parents, and program printing for school events)

Of course, you will need to search further after finding funders that share your general area of interest. Most funders also are interested in specific subject areas, such as technology, after-school programs, extended-school-year programs, and parenting training.

IDENTIFY CORPORATIONS THAT WANT TO HELP

Corporate funding is the easiest to obtain. How do you identify corporations that have financial assets to give your school cash or donated equipment or supplies? Here are some great sources for information on corporations and businesses in your local area:

- Local chamber of commerce membership lists contain contact information and classify businesses by category. Purchase a directory and use the information to develop mailing labels for selected businesses that have the potential to donate needed items or to write a check for your project needs.

- Regional economic development authority reports document top businesses and industries in your community and usually include key contact names, addresses, most recent profit or annual payroll, and number of employees. Such lists should be carefully examined, and might translate into corporate funding potential for the grant-searching detective. You can contact your local or regional economic development agency to request statistical reports.

- Local newspapers are full of information on local and regional corporations. Most newspapers have a business section where they list corporations in the state that are publicly traded. They might refer to these as the "Minnesota 100" or the "California 100" or the "Arkansas 10." This type of list will give you the names of major corporations in your state.

- State commerce and economic development Web sites are jackpots for finding new and existing corporations in your state.

Use the Internet in Your Research

Once you know the names of major corporations doing business in your locale or state, you can use the Internet to research their products, services, and their community involvement statement. Any corporation with a Web site link for "Community Involvement" or "Social Responsibility" is one that plans to give back monies to the areas where they do business and where their employees live.

You can retrieve more detailed information on corporations in your area or state by searching one of the several online subscription services—for example, Hoovers Online (www.hoovers online.com/free/). Also, remember to check with your public library for print directories, such as the *Thomas Register*™ or *Harris InfoSource*®.

SEEK OUT FOUNDATIONS

By nature, foundations are established to carry out the charitable missions of their donors. Many foundations are especially receptive to supporting all levels of education, from early childhood education through graduate study.

The Foundation Center

According to *Foundation Giving Trends*, published by the Foundation Center in 2003, education ranked first by share of foundation grant dollars. Foundations award billions of dollars annually for education programs—this includes K–12 schools! The Foundation Center is the premier source of nonprofit funding information. It collects data from corporate and foundation funders around the world and publishes profiles on them in books (*The Foundation Directory* and other specialized directories) and on the Internet (www.fdncenter.org). Some states have their own foundation directory, so check with your local public library to see if your state has one. Most states have at least one Foundation Center Cooperating Collection, which will be at a state university, community foundation, nonprofit resource center, or large public library. At these sites, you can use the Foundation Center publications, online subscription-based directory, and FC-Search CD-ROMs at no charge. Together, these information access tools contain more than 600,000 entries related to finding foundation grants.

STATE AND FEDERAL FUNDING AGENCIES FOR SCHOOLS

Grant announcements from federal agencies are published daily in the *Federal Register*. This document can be viewed at local libraries designated as Federal Depositories or can be found online at the U.S. Government Printing Office (GPO) Access Website (http://www.gpoaccess.gov/fr/index.html). The *Federal Register* lists all government business transactions, including grant funding or grant availability announcements.

FEDERAL FUNDING PROGRAMS

Can your school apply directly for federal grant monies? Yes, provided you use your school district as the grant applicant. Is this money different than the pass-through monies available through your state education agency? Yes, federal grant awards are viewed as a direct agreement between your school district and the federal agency doling out the grant money—usually the U.S. Department of Education. Recipients of "pass-through" grants are the state departments of education, even though the grant monies are subsequently distributed to local school districts in the form of formula allocations and competitive grant awards. The department provides more than $30 billion annually through formula-based grant programs and through direct competitive grant programs to improve elementary and secondary schools. The home Web page for this federal agency is www.ed.gov. When you view the site, remember to click on the "Grants & Contracts" link.

The Department of Education makes grant opportunities available to public and charter schools in academic and other areas, including:

- Carol M. White Physical Education Program

- Early Reading First Program

- Emergency response plans for school safety initiative

- Gifted and Talented Students Education Program

- Improving Literacy Through School Libraries Program

- Migrant Education Even Start Program

- Parental information resource centers

- School improvement foreign language assistance

- Teaching American history

The Department of Education also earmarks numerous grants for native Alaskans and Hawaiians and for federally recognized Indian tribes and tribal organizations. Check your state's department of education Web site frequently for competitive federal and state grant announcements (see page 6 for further details). The sooner you are aware of a grant funding opportunity, the sooner you or your school's grant writing team can start work on the grant application.

WINNING GOVERNMENT GRANTS

What are some of the things that give your school the edge for achieving government grants? If your school or school district is located in a specially designated federal zone, then your application will score more peer review points and knock out some of your competitors who lack the designation. When you submit your grant application package to a state or federal funding agency, federal legislation requires that your peers (other educators) participate in the decision-making process to fund or deny funding your grant request. Peer reviewers are oriented to the agency's grantmaking guidelines and give a copy of forms, titled Peer Review Forms. Each section in the narrative of your grant application as well as the budget section is assigned points. Most applications are assigned 100 points; some will have more points. Often you will see these points next to each section of the narrative in the grant application guidelines. For example, the need statement may be worth 20 points; the program design, 30 points. Peer reviewers are trained to look for specific guideline criteria in each section. If your application narrative adheres strictly to the guidelines, from formatting to competitive responses, then your application will score higher review points than other applications. Only applications with the highest review points are recommended for state or federal funding (this is covered in more detail on pages 26 and 27).

Empowerment Zone (EZ) and Enterprise Communities (EC). The Community Empowerment Program was enacted into law in August 1993. To be eligible, communities had to have high rates of poverty and submit an extensive application to the federal government. Urban and rural areas across the United States were selected to be federally designated Empowerment and Enterprise Zones. Each designation gives local communities special tax advantages to fuel economic development. In addition, every federal agency that bestows grants also gives extra technical review points to grant applicants located in an Empowerment or Enterprise Zone. If you are unsure of your community's status, call the local economic development agency and inquire—it is to your advantage to find out and use this "label" to attract government grant monies. You can also find a list of zone designations at this Web site: http://www.ed.gov/pubs/fixschools/zones.html. The site lists states, counties, and cities that qualify for special grant funding consideration.

Federal Colonias Zones. Colonias encompass communities of all types and sizes—both incorporated and unincorporated—that meet the federal definition of lacking sewer, wastewater, or decent housing. A "Colonia," Spanish for neighborhood or community, is a geographic area located within 150 miles of the U.S.-Mexico border that has a majority population composed of individuals and families of low and very low income. If your school is located near the U.S.-Mexico border, call your local U.S. Department of Housing and Urban Renewal (HUD) office to check your Colonias Zone status. Many government agencies add additional technical review points to your total grant application score if your school is located in one of these impoverished areas. This Web site provides links to regional U.S. Department of

Housing and Urban Development offices: http://www.hud. gov/
directory/ascdir3.cfm.

LESSONS LEARNED

Several years ago, soon after the EZs and ECs were established,
I wrote a federal grant application for a school corporation
located in a large EZ area, and this meant they had all the right
demographics for ranking high with the agency's peer reviewers
and program staff. The competition was stiff and fewer than 10
awards would be made nationally, but my client thankfully
received more than $800,000 in grant monies to start an alterna-
tive school for dropouts. Later, a Congressional member from my
client's state told me that the EZ designation made all the difference in the world for achieving this grant.

ACTION STEPS

Search daily. Set aside a time every day to search for grant funding opportunities. Check your mail and e-mail for announcements. Read the newspaper, looking for new businesses moving into the state or region. Log onto the Internet and check your state education agency, U.S. Department of Education, and Foundation Center Web sites. Share your findings with members of your grant writing team.

Be creative. If you cannot find anything relevant to your school's needs, then try using a search engine, such as Google™ (www.google.com), and type in "math grants," "computer grants," "science grants," "consumer science grants," "grants for elementary schools," and so forth in the search box.

Surf with the pros. Log onto the Web site Welcome to School Grants! (www.schoolgrants.org) and see what you have been missing. Your peers around the country use this free Web site to identify all types of school grants, and to see examples of funded grant applications posted by teachers who have been successful at winning grants for their schools.

Chapter 3

Learning the Lingo
to Trump the Competition

UNDERSTANDING STANDARD GRANT-RELATED LINGO will help you sail through funding agency guidelines and decide if the grant opportunity is right for your school. Every weekday, funding agencies issue grant availability announcements and requests for proposals. You need to be ready to take action as soon as the guidelines are released on the Internet or sent to your school's key administrative contacts. As a grant writer for your school, once you grasp the lingo—the vocabulary of the grant writing field—you will hit the ground running whenever an announcement comes your way. You will be able to read and understand the technical requirements of the grant application or proposal guidelines and immediately start formulating a response. You will be able to trump the competition!

Many readers might already be familiar with some of the grant-related terms covered in this chapter, but please do not skip it. Even teachers who are veteran grant writers can use a refresher.

BASIC GRANT-RELATED TERMINOLOGY

Grant—a monetary award given to a qualifying agency or individual. All grant awards have usage and spending stipulations. Inappropriately used grant monies may be viewed as disallowed costs or expenditures by a funder and could result in the grant being revoked. In other words, if your school or district does not comply with all stipulations, it might have to return 100% of the grant award.

Competitive grant—a monetary award given to an eligible applicant who has competed successfully against other eligible applicants for a limited number of grant awards. The grant competition may be open to local, regional, and/or national applicants. The more widespread the competition, the fewer chances there are of winning a grant award—unless you have submitted a well-written grant application!

Formula grant—a monetary award based on an allocation formula (for schools, this is usually the annual pupil head count). Schools filling out the proper forms automatically receive formula grants. These applications are referred to as "no-brainers," meaning they require no research and very little writing time. Yet many small and/or rural school districts tend to overlook the forms when they arrive in the mail or simply do not take the time to sign on the bottom line and return them to the state education agency.

GUIDELINE AND APPLICATION TERMINOLOGY

Catalog of Federal Domestic Assistance (CFDA) number—a number assigned by the federal agency administering the monies earmarked for contract and grant awards and used to identify a specific program. The agency publishes the CFDA number along with the funding program description in the *Federal Register* (see page 16 for further details) or on its Web site.

Purpose—a statement describing what grant monies must be used for. The purpose usually contains key buzzwords that should be incorporated into the grant application or proposal narrative.

Due date—day and time when the grant application must be received by the funding agency. Always, always submit your grant application or proposal 48 hours before the due date—*no exceptions*. Unforeseen things happen and you do not want to work so hard to put your vision in writing only to miss the due date!

Allocation—the amount of money the funding agency has designated, or earmarked, for the grant program.

Priority—concerns that must be addressed in the grant application in order for the proposed project to be recommended for a grant award. Priority areas usually follow the purpose section in funding guidelines.

Cover page, assurances, and partner sign-off forms—standard forms, complete with detailed instructions, found in all state and federal grant application kits or guidelines. Contact information and an overview of the proposed project go on the cover page. In the assurances, you verify that your organization has the capacity to conduct the project. The partner sign-off form provides documentation for the grant reviewer regarding the other organizations involved in the project. These forms will require the signature of your district's superintendent or chief administrator. Original signatures (before you make copies for the funder) must be in *blue* ink.

Abstract—a one-page summary that briefly describes the project's vision, goals, activities, key features that will be addressed, and the expected benefits of the project. Some funders provide a form to be filled out for the abstract.

Program narrative—a clear and concise project description based on the funder's purpose and priorities. This section usually has a page limit and includes instructions on font style and line spacing. You must follow the narrative formatting instructions exactly. Deviating from the instructions could result in your grant application not being reviewed by the funder.

Budget summary and detail—a description of the exact cost of implementing the project and a justification for certain line items. You will want to work closely with your district's business office or finance officer to nail down the numbers for this section.

Attachments or appendix—additional documentation supporting the plans presented in the program narrative. Documents may include letters of commitment from school partners, résumés of key faculty and staff, elaboration of data used to establish the need, evidence of impact from prior grant funding efforts for this and similar projects, and elaboration of the research or evidence bases used to design the program.

TECHNICAL TERMINOLOGY

Review process—the scrutiny a grant application or proposal undergoes once the funder receives it and logs it in. The process includes a technical review and a peer review.

Technical review—the first review in the review process. If you failed to include a grant application original document (with the blue signature) and the requested number of copies, your application will not meet the technical review. If you failed to include mandatory forms and attachments, your application will not meet the technical review. If you missed the grant application deadline, your application will not meet the technical review. Applications passing the technical review move on to the peer review.

Peer Review—the second part of the review process in which your peers—other educators—get together to read and discuss your grant application to determine how well your project meets the criteria for the grant competition. The peer reviewers apply a numerical scoring system to each grant application. The system is based on criteria that support the funder's purpose and priorities. Some grant applications have 100 review points; others will have more depending on the number of priorities. The reality of the situation is that your grant application needs to score 90 points or higher to be recommended for funding by the peer review panel. Table 3.1 shows a sample of review criteria for the peer review.

Table 3.1

Sample Peer Review Criteria

Criteria	Points
Demonstration of need	15
Research or evidence base	15
Plan of work	20
Management capability	10
Sustainability	10
Evaluation plan	15
Budget summary and detail	15
Total Possible Review Points	**100**

Unallowable costs—costs that cannot be covered with grant award monies. Tuition charges, entertainment, and capital or nonexpendable supply equipment are examples of unallowable costs by funders.

Nonexpendable equipment expenditures—an item is nonexpendable if it is damaged or some of its parts are lost or worn out, and it is more feasible to repair the item than to replace it with an entirely new unit. Under normal conditions of use, including reasonable care and maintenance, it can be expected to serve its principal purpose for at least one year.

LESSONS LEARNED

Before the Internet was widely accessible, I used to spend hours at the local public library and the university government documents collection library finding and studying grant announcements. What was I trying to do? Learn the lingo and find public and private grant funding opportunities. Today, it is so easy to search the Internet for the definitions of technical terms, examples of completed grant proposals and applications, and online newsletters that use the lingo (or "grantology" as I like to call it) to report the latest funding news to their subscribers. The most important thing you can do to familiarize yourself with grant-related terms is to read all of the electronic and print publications you can find on grant writing, grant management, and funding opportunities.

ACTION STEPS

Obtain the guidelines. Every funder has grant application or proposal submission guidelines. Do your homework and get the guidelines as soon as you find out about the availability of grant funds.

Read the guidelines. Read the grant application guidelines several times. First, read for the basics: purpose, priority, amount of money to be awarded, number of grants to be awarded, and due date. Second, read for technical requirements: required forms and attachments, sign-offs needed from partners, administrative signatories, research required, length of narrative, and font and line spacing specifications. Third, read for preparing to write. Ask yourself what each section of the narrative calls for and where you will get the information to write each section.

Highlight the guidelines. Highlight any technical detail that could result in your grant application being rejected during the technical review process. Are you required to first send a letter to the funder stating your district intends to apply for grant funds? Is there a deadline for this letter? Are you required to submit a copy of your completed grant application to a regional planning organization for public comment? Are you required to hold public meetings prior to submitting the grant application? Tab the grant application kit pages you highlighted so you can quickly refer to what must be done.

Chapter 4

Is the Game Worth Playing?

IT IS CRITICAL TO MATCH THE RIGHT FUNDER to your project if you want to hit the target the first time in your grant seeking efforts. Remember, you will always need external funding support—the key is to start early by identifying funding partners whose grantmaking areas match your school's or district's needs.

GATHERING INFORMATION

Figure 4.1 (beginning on page 33) can be used as a prospect research worksheet for foundations or corporations. Gathering the qualifying information on the worksheets will help you select the grant makers most likely to fund your project.

When you follow up on a funding alert from a foundation or corporation or when you identify these types of funding opportunities using the Internet, you need a way to track your findings and to qualify the funder. In other words, you need to capture the most critical information about the funder in order to determine if it is a strong contender for receiving a grant proposal from your school district.

After you have filled in three to five prospect worksheets for your project, you can review them over and over to target the best of the bunch. Once you or your grant writing team have selected the top one or two funders, you can proceed with preparing to apply. Remember, some funders want to see a letter of inquiry first, before you submit a full unsolicited grant proposal for their review.

WINNING A GOVERNMENT AGENCY AWARD

Remember, your chances for winning a government agency grant award are always better if you apply for your state's department of education grant opportunities. There will be times when federal grant announcements look appealing, but before you take the leap into federal grant writing, you need to answer the prequalifying questions as outlined in Table 4.1 (page 36).

Some federal grant monies have set-asides (money that is set aside out of the total pool of grant funds available) for U.S. territories, Native American tribes, and faith-based organizations. This means there will be fewer funds for competitive grant making. Always read every sentence in a grant application announcement because some federal agencies issue grant announcements for specific states or territories (this is defined as a *funding limitation*). Funding limitation means that if your geographic location is not included in the "invitation to apply for grant funds," you would be wasting your time to proceed with writing the grant application.

If no other schools in your state have ever received a grant award from a particular government funding agency, this can be good for your school. You can point out to your Congressional team member that your state has been left out of the funding

(continued on page 37)

Figure 4.1

Prospect Research Worksheet
for Foundations and Corporations

Name: _____

Contact Person/Title: _____

Address: _____

City: _____ State: _____ Zip Code: _____

Telephone: _____

E-mail: _____

Web Site Address: _____

Number of Employees (if applicable): _____

Year Founded: _____

Donors: _____

Products/Services (if applicable): _____

_____

_____

Foundation Type:
   ___Independent

   ___Community Foundation

   ___Corporate/Company Sponsored

   ___Corporate Giving Program

Total Assets: _____

Gifts Received: _____

Total Grants: _____

Grant Ranges: _____

Period of Funding: _____

Subject Focus (list in order of importance):_____

_____

_____

Geographic Limitations: _____

_____

_____

Population Group(s) Served: _____

_____

_____

Type(s) of Support:_____

_____

_____

Type(s) of Recipient(s):_____

_____

_____

Personnel (chairman, chief executive officer, other officers and
directors, staff): _____

_____

_____

_____

_____

Application Requirements: _____

_____

_____

_____

_____

Printed Guidelines?   ___Yes   ___No

Deadline: _____

Board Meeting Date(s):_____

_____

Initial Approach (letter of inquiry, formal proposal):_____

Reasons This Foundation or Corporation Would Want to Fund Your School: _____

_____
_____
_____
_____
_____
_____

Restrictions on Funding: _____

_____
_____
_____
_____
_____

Comments: _____

_____
_____
_____
_____
_____

Research Prepared By: _____
Date: _____

Table 4.1

Qualifying Checklist

GUIDING QUESTIONS	YES	NO
Applicant eligibility—Is my school district eligible to apply?		
Internal capacity—When is the deadline for the application and can we meet it?		
Alignment with school improvement and reform initiatives—Does the grant meet the funding priorities that the school or district established in its planning process?		
Sustainability—Is this a service or activity my school district can continue to fund out of district monies once the grant funding is gone?		
Set-asides and limitations—What is the competition like?		
Worthy effort—How much money is available?		
Geographic advantage—Is there a geographic restriction, and did any other school districts in our state receive this grant money in previous funding years?		
Bull's-eye targeting—Does our idea for a grant request match the funding agency's guidelines and interest?		

loop. If other schools have previously received grant awards, look at their locations. Are they in your county? Are they in your town? If so, there is a strong probability that a federal grant may not be awarded in the same locale for a year or more. Federal grants are disbursed geographically throughout the United States and its territories. No one area can be over saturated.

WEIGHING OPTIONS

If you answer no to any of the questions on the checklist, then you need to (a) reconvene your grant writing team to discuss uncertainties and (b) call the funding agency to obtain answers to questions that would clear up your uncertainties. The following advice from educators experienced in writing winning grant applications may help you tackle problems with grant opportunities:

- If your school or district cannot be the grant applicant, then look for a community partner, such as a college or university, or even a human services coordinating council to act as the grant applicant and funding partner.

- If your grant writing team cannot meet a short deadline requirement, then consider asking your administrator to contract with a freelance grant writing consultant.

- Do not chase after grants for the sake of getting a grant award if the funds do not align with the goals and objectives in your school improvement plan or technology plan.

- Remember, not all schools or districts have the capacity to accept a large government grant that requires matching funds or that stipulates your district's ongoing fiscal responsibility to maintain the grant-funded program after the grant award has been expended.

- Until you have moved from novice (just starting to learn the grant writing process) to veteran status (when closer to 100% of your submitted proposals are funded), avoid expending your energy on federal grant competitions where ten or fewer grants are going to be awarded. First, hone your skills and track your successes. Second, look for grant announcements where at least one award will be made in each state. The more awards, the higher your chances are of winning one for your school district. When I gamble on a long shot in the grant seeking game, I make sure my client is located in a set-aside area, has a federal economically distressed designation, and has student and parent demographics that will inspire sympathy in the peer reviewers.

- If you need $500,000 and the grant award range is $50,000 to $100,000, consider downscaling your program and budget so that $100,000 will start a pilot program. If you cannot downscale to $100,000, then this particular grant competition may not be appropriate for your school.

- Carefully read the fine print in all government grant announcements. Some federal grants specify which states or regions can apply for competitive grant funds. Avoid the huge disappointment of becoming excited about a grant opportunity announcement only to find out after 50 hours of planning and research that your state is not on the list of states that can apply for the grant funds.

- Carefully read the grant guidelines. Make sure your idea or program aligns with the funding agency's criteria of what they want to fund. Funders do not change their priorities—you and your grant writing team have to redesign your vision to fit the funding priority.

LESSONS LEARNED

Whenever I am going to write a grant application to a state or federal funding agency, I always telephone or e-mail the contact person for the grant program. Why? First, I want to establish a personal connection between the funder's staff and the community in need of the grant monies. By creating an ally, I am giving my grant application a higher recognition level in the grant seeking game. Second, I want to be alerted via e-mail to any technical assistance workshops planned in my region so I can attend and speak with program staff one-to-one. This is another advantage in the government grant seeking game. Third, when I am down to the last hour and have urgent technical questions, I know someone at the funding agency to e-mail or call to either talk with immediately or receive an expedited response by other means.

(continued)

ACTION STEPS

Customize your checklist. Work with your grant writing team to develop a "Grant Writing Preplanning Checklist" that better fits your school's needs. If you are a grant coordinator for your district, then you will want to draft a prescreening form for district grant seekers that enables you to determine if the funding fits the need.

Always invite your financial officer to your meetings. When you schedule a meeting to review the grant application guidelines and requirements, make sure to invite your district's chief financial officer or business manager. Convey to him or her the urgency of helping you review the proposed budget, matching funds requirements, and sustainability requirements.

Use existing planning documents to guide you. Every grant application you agree to write must fit a priority or need in the school's or district's long-range plan. This plan could be your school improvement plan or the technology plan. The goals and objectives in the application you prepare will be based on the same goals and objectives found in the long-range plan.

Chapter 5

Getting Into the Grant Writing Game: Letters to Funders

As you research corporate and foundation funders, you will find that many of them want a letter of inquiry or a letter proposal instead of a full grant proposal. What do they want to read about? Funders want to read relevant information concerning your school and district, the problem that needs a solution, and, of course, the project that matches their area of interest. You should present your vision in a friendly, easy-to-read format:

- Print letter on school or district letterhead.

- Use wide margins on all sides.

- Use a 12-point font that is not too decorative or unusual.

- Format text as ragged right. (Do not justify it on the right margin. This is a sore point with many grant readers and reviewers.)

- Use single spacing within paragraphs and double spacing between paragraphs.

- Limit the letter to one page.

Last but not least, remember to provide the signatory with a draft of the letter for his or her feedback and approval before sending off the final letter.

COVER LETTERS

All grant proposal documents, including state and federal grant applications, need a cover letter. Cover letters highlight the contents of the proposal and are the first impression the reviewer has of your organization and its need. Here are the elements of a cover letter:

- **Date**

- **Inside address**
  Contact name, title, funder name and full address.

- **Regarding**
  For corporations and foundations, enter your project name; for state agencies, enter the name of the grant competition; and for federal agencies, enter the CFDA number.

- **Dear** _____:
  Make sure you know the correct spelling of the contact person's name and which courtesy title to use. *Always use a colon after the contact's last name; never use a comma.*

- **Opening paragraph**
  Give the grant applicant's full proper name and indicate you are submitting this request for funder review. Mention that you look forward to your partnership with the funded grant program.

- **Second paragraph**

  Include the statement: "This proposal requests $_____ to (_describe to the funder what receipt of project grant monies will enable your school or district to do_) from the (_give the name of the funding agency_)." This is where you tell the funder about your school's or district's unmet needs.

- **Third paragraph**

  Provide some general information about your school or district. For example: your enrollment, rural or urban location, special circumstances, or federal designations.

- **Final paragraph**

  Thank the funder in advance for reviewing your proposal and considering a partnership that will enable (_name your target population for the grant funds_) to achieve (_enter the funder's vision or priority for funding_). End this paragraph with an upbeat statement.

- **Closing**

  Sign off with "Sincerely," "Hopefully," "Respectfully," or the complimentary close of your choice.

- **Signature**

  Have the district superintendent or authorized building administrator sign the letter.

If you decide to work with a freelance grant writer, make sure that the task of preparing the cover letter remains the responsibility of the school district. Cover letters need to have a personal touch and not be a reiteration of the grant proposal request.

LETTERS OF INQUIRY

Many foundations prefer that you first approach them by submitting a letter of inquiry—basically a "mini-concept" paper in letter format. After reviewing your letter of inquiry, the funder decides whether or not to ask your school or district to submit a full grant proposal. If the funder is not interested in funding your project, you will receive a standard-form rejection letter. However, if the funder is interested in possibly funding your project, you will receive an invitation to send in a full project description.

You can increase the odds of getting in the grant game when you do homework on funders instead of sending out letters haphazardly. Always research funding sources on the Internet; then call or e-mail them to request copies of their annual reports. Armed with such information, you will make inquiries only to grantmakers currently interested in projects like yours.

Write an Inquiry That Will Gain Notice

How do you write a compelling letter of inquiry? Such a convincing letter has these elements:

- **Date**

- **Inside address**
  Contact name, title, funder name, and full address.

- **Dear** _____:
  Make sure you know the correct spelling of the contact person's name and which courtesy title to use. *Always use a colon after the contact's last name; never use a comma.*

- **Opening paragraph**

  Introduce your school *and* district to the funder. Tell the funder your organization's full legal name, where it is located, and its most recent client service numbers. Include demographics about your target population.

- **Letter body**

  Briefly describe the project or program you need funding for and the amount requested. Tell the funder why these needs have gone unmet and state why you are approaching this particular funder.

- **Closing paragraph**

  Write a closing paragraph to thank the funder for their time and for considering asking you to submit a full grant proposal.

- **Closing**

  Sign off with "Sincerely," "Hopefully," "Respectfully," or the complimentary close of your choice.

- **Signature**

  Have your district superintendent or authorized building administrator sign the letter.

- **Attachments**

  Attach the full project budget with detailed line items.

The formatting for letters of inquiry should always be single-spaced paragraphs with double spacing between paragraphs. Do not exceed the number of pages specified by the funder in their guidelines for your letter of inquiry.

LETTER PROPOSALS

You might ask yourself, "Who wants to receive a letter proposal?" Corporations, small businesses, and smaller foundations prefer to receive a three-page letter proposal instead of a full five-page grant proposal. Why? These types of grantmakers have limited staff to review the daily mailbag of funding requests. Often fewer than two staff persons are answering the telephones, opening mail, reviewing funding requests, sorting the requests by funder priority area, and making recommendations to the board of directors or trustees. In other words, like teachers, the funder's staff wears multiple hats. A letter proposal gives funders just enough information to make a positive decision, but not enough to overwhelm them with infinite detail.

Write Less to Win More

With a letter proposal, you succinctly present your project for funding consideration. Because corporate and foundation funders do not use peer review teams or a point-based rating system, you must grab the program officer's attention to be given consideration for any grant money during the fiscal year. A letter proposal includes these elements:

- **Date**

- **Inside address**
  Contact name, title, funder name and full address.

- **Dear** _____:
  Make sure you know the correct spelling of the contact person's name and which courtesy title to use. *Always use a colon after the contact's last name; never use a comma.*

- **Opening paragraph**

  The first words in your opening paragraph are the "bait" for your potential funder. You plant the bait by writing three bulleted sentences about your target population and why they are at risk. Focus on risk factors related to the proposal request. The intent of these one-liner "calls for help" is to reel in your reader and get him or her to read the rest of the letter.

- **Letter body**

  State your problem (unmet needs) in two to three paragraphs.

  - Introduce your school and district and include the mission statement. (If this request will only benefit a single school within a district, then give the school's mission statement.)

  - Write a detailed description of the project. Include your purpose statement, goals, and measurable objectives, as well as a timeline for when the objectives will be achieved. State the amount of funding requested and how the funder can help solve the problem. Give demographics on your target population. Make sure to tell the funder if this is a new or existing project. If it is an existing project, state where current funding comes from (names of sources and amount each awards annually).

  - Write about your community partners and their roles in and contributions to the project. Specify whether the support is monetary or in-kind.

- Present a brief overview of project staff and talk about the role played by volunteers, especially parents. Include numbers of staff and volunteers and how many hours each group will commit annually to the project. This information is noteworthy, since the national hourly value of a volunteer's time exceeds $16. *Volunteer hours count as in-kind or matching contributions when applying for grants.*

- Offer a plan for monitoring and evaluating the progress of the project's objectives. State who (individual, team, or third-party agency) will be responsible for developing the evaluation plan. Tell the funder how you will share the findings from your evaluation with other schools, districts, and educators outside of your district. You may want to say you will present "white papers" (a project overview or summary) at regional and national education conferences.

- List the district's human, financial, and physical resources that will be committed to the project, indicating the total value of cash resources and in-kind resources. Also list the names of other funders who will receive proposals for the project. Tell the funder how your project will be sustained once the grant has ended.

- **Closing paragraph**
  Thank the funder for their time and consideration of your proposal.

- **Closing**

  Sign off with "Sincerely," "Hopefully," "Respectfully," or the complimentary close of your choice.

- **Signatory**

  Have your district superintendent or authorized building administrator sign the letter.

- **Attachments**

  Include with your letter:

  - Full project budget with detailed line items

  - Current district or school-level operating budget

  - List of board of education members or trustees that includes the following information for each individual: name, board position, occupation in community, gender, and ethnicity

  - Letters from parents and community partners to support the need for the project

LESSONS LEARNED

During my early days of grant writing, I always wrote a full grant proposal to send to funders. I never paid attention to the letter of inquiry requirement. However, I also noticed that my funding success rate was declining, and I received more rejections than grant awards. Nowadays, if the funder prefers to have a letter of inquiry first before reviewing a full grant proposal, I always prepare one. My funding success rate now ranges between 90% and 95% on all projects. It is worth it to pay attention to what each funder wants to see first: letter of inquiry, letter proposal, or proposal.

WAIT PATIENTLY

Most funders receive hundreds of unsolicited grant proposals every week. Even funders with large staffs have a difficult time logging in all of the proposals and assigning them to the various program officers. Your proposal could sit on a program officer's desk for months before being opened and reviewed.

The longest waiting period I ever endured was 18 months. By the time the check for $10,000 arrived on the school superintendent's desk, he had forgotten what the school had asked for. It took a quick call to me to refresh his memory. We had requested $10,000 for drama props and stage upgrades in the district's auditorium. Good thing he asked—thinking there was a mistake, he was ready to send the check back!

IF YOU RECEIVE BAD NEWS

No one likes to receive a standard-form rejection letter, postcard, or e-mail, but if your letter proposal is rejected you will not have to wait long to learn the results—typically, you will be notified within 6 months from the date you mailed it to the funder. It is acceptable to call or write the funder to inquire about why your proposal was not selected for funding recommendation, but do not expect much, if any, detailed feedback on the reason for rejection. Bad news means you need to start over and do it better the next time. I advise my clients to call funders that have sent them rejection letters and inquire about why the proposal was not funded. Often this valuable one-on-one feedback opens the door to resubmit a more specific or even an entirely different funding request. One client in particular was denied funding for what I felt was a very well matched and worthy project. However, when she called the funder to inquire about the rejection, she was invited to reapply for a different project—one that the funder felt better matched their not yet announced area of interest.

IF YOU RECEIVE GOOD NEWS

It could take up to 18 months for you to receive a positive response to a letter proposal, but the good news is that when you get the award letter it will come with a check enclosed. At that time, arrange to have your board of education prepare a certificate of appreciation and thank you letter for the funder.

PARTNERSHIP ETIQUETTE

Once a corporation or foundation funds your project, they become your partner. Keeping your funding partner updated on how grant monies are expended and on project evaluation findings will build goodwill that will extend far beyond the funding period. If the funder is located nearby, invite them to visit your school and see the impact of their financial investment for themselves. You should also put together a scrapbook with pictures, articles, letters of appreciation from students and parents, and other outcome-supporting documentation that you can give to funders at the end of the funding period as evidence of project success.

(continued)

ACTION STEPS

Seek administrative approval. Before you start looking for external funding support from corporations, foundations, and state and federal agencies, make sure your superintendent approves your efforts and is willing to allocate time during the school day for you to proceed with grant seeking. Keeping your superintendent informed as you prepare one of these letters ensures that there will not be any disappointments or surprises when the time comes to sign and mail it.

Enlist a colleague as your editor. Almost all writers are blind to their own mistakes. Find a colleague who is willing to edit and proof all of your letters before you take them to the superintendent for signature, and especially before you mail them to the funder.

Track the status of all letters. Create a database or spreadsheet file on your computer to record the dates you write, sign, and mail each letter and to record the status of this correspondence with each funder.

Chapter 6

Winning Foundation Grant Proposals

YOU MUST PLAY BY FOUNDATION RULES TO WIN A GRANT. The
tricky part is determining which grant proposal rules to follow.
Some foundations have their own grant application forms while
others require a customized cover form to be used instead of your
own standard proposal format. Some foundations indicate in
their published guidelines that they want proposals in either the
Regional Association of Grantmakers (RAGs) format or the
National Network of Grantmakers (NNG) format. Most foundations accept the NNG format.

Remember, grants awards are competitive. How can foundations eliminate the stacks of unsolicited and solicited proposals
dumped into their mailboxes every day? By requiring grant seekers
to jump through a lot of technical hoops. Grant seekers who "do
their own thing" when it comes to submitting a proposal to a foundation will quickly find themselves on the standard-form rejection
letter recipient list. Another tactic used to reduce the number of
funding requests is requiring customized application forms. For
example, many foundations require scanning of the forms, then typing in the requested information—a tedious process. Other foundations want your entire request limited to a one-page application

form with no attachments. The key is to never, ever send the same generic proposal to all of the foundations you approach. This is called "funding suicide," and you cannot go back to these funders for years if you make this mistake!

A funding agency can quickly identify grant proposals that are part of a "shotgun" or "blanket" mailing: the same proposal sent to multiple funders with no changes to customize the request. Your school will not only receive a rejection letter, but any future attempts to obtain funding will be quickly thwarted by the funding staff that never forgets your generic request.

RAG APPLICATION FORMAT

You can check to see if your state has a RAG format by logging onto the Giving Forum of the Regional Association of Grantmakers Web site (http://www.givingforum.org/index.html). Click on "About RAGs," and then click on the "Regional Association Locator" in the left column. Continue following the links until you pull up the screen for the RAG in your state. Next, look for a link to their Common Grant Application. If you do not find one, you should use the NNG Common Grant Application format for your foundation proposal. You can download a template of the NNG common grant application form at the National Network of Grantmakers' Web site (www.nng.org).

NNG COMMON GRANT APPLICATION

The Common Grant Application was created by the National Network of Grantmakers in 1995 for groups seeking grants for social and economic justice work. However, since its creation the format has been widely used by grant writers seeking funds in a range of disciplines. The application is a concise, standard format that gives any foundation funder just enough of the necessary information to make a positive funding decision. Hundreds of U.S. foundations are familiar with this writer/reader-friendly format. If they do not have their own customized grant application form, these foundations will readily accept and review proposals written in the NNG format.

The NNG format consists of four main sections: a cover letter, a cover sheet, the grant application narrative (maximum five single-spaced pages, with double-spacing between paragraphs), and attachments. Your project budget must be formatted using the NNG Budget Form. Organizational and key personnel information is included in the attachments. Attachments are discussed on pages 71–77 in extensive detail.

Cover letter. Cover letters for foundation proposals follow the format discussed in chapter 5 (see page 42). Your cover letter should not be longer than one page and should have 1-inch margins. You will not want to give the grant reviewer too much information—just enough to entice him or her to read the grant proposal narrative.

Cover Sheet. The cover sheet is also limited to one page, with at least 1-inch margins on all sides. You can make it easier to read by double-spacing between the lines. If you want to add a border to dress up the cover sheet, choose a simple one—do not make the cover sheet look like a picture frame crammed full of text.

The following section outlines the elements of a cover sheet. Please note some of the wording has been modified from the NNG format to make the form more applicable to schools. The text in brackets provides examples of information that would go in that particular field.

I. COMMON GRANT COVER SHEET

- Grant applicant's name [full name of school or district]

- Type of school [grade levels, public or private, elementary, middle, or high school]

- Year school was organized

- Date of application

- Address

- Telephone number

- Fax number

- Superintendent

- Contact person and title [if different than superintendent]

- Grant request

- Period grant will cover

- Type of request [general support, start-up, technical assistance, and so on]

- Project title [if project funding is requested]

- Total project budget [if request is for something other than general support]

- Total district budget [for the current year]

- Starting date of fiscal year

- Summary of the district's mission [limit your comments to two or three sentences]

- Summary of project or grant request [limit your comments to two or three sentences]

Grant application narrative. The Common Grant Application narrative is divided into two distinct sections. Part A requests information on the applicant organization—that is your school or district. Part B requests information about your proposed project or program. Again you will single-space your paragraphs and double-space between paragraphs. Because you will want to make your information visually appealing to the grant reviewer, select a font that is reader-friendly, such as Times New Roman, Arial, or Gill Sans MT. <u>Never use Courier!</u> Courier resembles the common, everyday typewriter font. It is viewed as too plain and does nothing to encourage the grant reviewer to eagerly read the next sentence, paragraph, or page. To draw attention to important information, use bullets to set off separate subsections under each primary section.

Most of the rest of this chapter illustrates the format for the narrative and the program evaluation. Please note that the subsection headings are modified to make this format more applicable to schools. After each subsection heading, under the rubrics *Primer, Recommended Length,* and *Visual Enhancements,* helpful advice is given on the type of information the funder is looking for when reviewing your grant proposal.

II. NARRATIVE (maximum of five pages)

A. Introduction and Background of Organization [incorporate the following points]

1. Grant applicant's history and major accomplishments

Primer. In this subsection, give the grant reviewer the full legal name of your school district; your geographic location (city, county, and state); number of years established; and major proposal-related accomplishments. In other words, unless you are requesting grant funds for a scoreboard for the school's athletic complex, do not tout your sport accolades. Focus instead on academic accomplishments.

Recommended length. Provide one short paragraph for this subsection.

Visual enhancements. Insert a regional or state map, using a star or arrow to point to your school's location. A subtle way of including a graphic without taking up space needed for narrative text is to make the graphic a watermark. Check your word-processing manual for instructions.

2. Description of current programs and activities

Primer. In this subsection, describe all of the academic programs offered at your school, ranging from preschool programs to gifted and talented programs to school-to-work programs. If your school is involved in any academic Olympics programs, share this with the grant reviewer and talk about the number of times or events your school has captured academic recognition, including awards.

Recommended length. This subsection should be one short paragraph. You can always create a one-page school or district program fact sheet and add it to the attachments. If you opt to make a fact sheet, be sure to reference it in this subsection. For example: "These are only a few of the many academic programs offered at the Hillside School District. A complete list of programs and activities is included in the **Attachments.**" Be sure to boldface the word *attachments* to draw the grant reviewer's attention to your supporting documentation and its location.

Visual enhancements. Use no graphics in this subsection.

3. Community and school demographics

Primer. In this subsection, provide the grant reviewer with current demographics on the community and the students the school serves. This information should not be more than 5 years old. The best way to present demographics is by creating a table with key indicators. The table on the next page is an example.

Your table should extend to the right and left margins and should not take up more than a third of a page. The time-span comparison should be at least 3 years apart, but should not go back beyond 5 years. You can request school-related statistics from the district's central office or find them in your school's report card on your state department of education's Web site. Community indicators can be collected from the police or sheriff's department, local or regional economic development agency, newspaper articles, the Kids

Table 1

Hillside's Stakeholders

Indicator	2000	2004	Impact on District's Capacity
K-12 enrollment			
Teacher-to-pupil ratio			*Insert comparison information and its resulting impact here.*
Title I (low-income) eligible students			
Dropout rate			
Graduation rate			
Percent of students retained at same grade level (failed to pass)			
Percent of students failing proficiency level on state reading test			
Percent of students failing proficiency on state mathematics test			
Percent of minority students			
Number of students residing in single-parent households			
Unemployment rate			
Juvenile crime rate			
(Add other indicators as needed)			

Count Web site at www.aecf.org/kidscount/, and employment bureau or the local workforce development office.

End this subsection by telling the grant reviewer how your stakeholders are actively involved in school or district activities and how they benefit from their involvement. For example, write about the number of parents who volunteer their time to help at their child's school. Write about how business people speak at career day or how employers support employees mentoring or tutoring students in school programs. Be sure to write about senior citizens who donate their time to share a hobby or teach a vintage craft. Most importantly, summarize the overall benefits of community involvement in your school—for the community and for the students.

Recommended length. Limit your table and narrative to one-half page.

Visual enhancements. The table provides a visual break in the grant reviewer's narrative reading. Add 10% gray shading to the table's headings row. Add no other graphics to this subsection.

4. Community and regional partnerships

Primer. You can put this subsection's information in table format. If you think that having two tables back to back must be taboo, there is no need to worry. Grant reviewers appreciate seeing important information presented clearly and concisely in tables. At this point in your grant application narrative, you should be at the top of page 2. This position is not a suggestion, but a *firm directive*. You will need at least three pages (all that are remaining in the five-page limit) to write Part B. Here is an example of how to present the partnership information in a table:

Table 2

School or District Partnerships

Community Partner	Role With School or District
Hillside Chamber of Commerce	*Name your partners and list their roles in your school's or district's programs.*
Hillside PTO	
Hillside University	
Human Services Coordinating Council	
Regional Educational Media Center	

Recommended length. Use no more than one-third page for this table.

Visual enhancements. Add 10% gray shading to the headings row. Do not add more graphics or tables in this section.

B. Description of the District's or School's Request [incorporate the following points]

1. Problem statement

Primer. In this subsection, you provide the grant reviewer with well-researched information on the problem, need, or issue that grant monies will address. This is not the section to reveal your solution. This is the section to write about the gloom, doom, drama, and trauma, which is supported by cited references. You want the grant reviewer to sit up, pay attention, and take note of your grim circumstances—circumstances that can only be improved with grant funding support. If you are unable to come up with any language to describe the distressing situation at your school or district, you may not need grant funding. Some compelling descriptive factors might be:

- Academics—the students have experienced academic failure in preceding years

- Economics—the students come from poor economic circumstances

- Remoteness—the students come from small, rural, or inaccessible communities

- Underachievement—the students have been unable to realize minimal proficiencies

- Anxiety—the students succumb to pressure from their peers

- Defeat—the students may feel that they will not graduate because their parents and other relatives did not achieve graduation

Recommended length. This subsection will likely start on the bottom half of page 2 of your Common Grant Application narrative and should extend to the middle of page 3. If you do not build a strong case for need, a smooth program design will not matter because you will have already lost the grant reviewer's attention in the problem statement.

Visual enhancements. Use boldface and underlining to highlight key heart-rending phrases. For example: "In 2003, **24 percent** of fifth graders <u>failed to test at the minimal proficiency level</u> on Oregon's State Assessment for Life Sciences."

2. Purpose of grant funding request

Primer. In this subsection get right to the point with the grant reviewer. Start this section with the following sentence: "The purpose of this grant request is to seek $_____ from the *(name of funding agency)* for the *(insert project name here)*." The project name your grant writing team selects should have a suitable acronym that will not be offensive to the grant reviewer or others. The second and final sentence of this subsection should tell the grant reviewer if this project is a new or an ongoing activity of your school or district.

Recommended length. Limit your response to two sentences.

Visual enhancements. Use no graphics in this subsection.

3. Goals, objectives, activities/strategies, and timelines

Primer. You may find this hard to believe, but some grant writers go astray when writing goals and objectives. There is a distinction between the two terms.

Goals are the visionary, global, futuristic end-of-funding outcomes for your grant proposal's target population. *Goals are not written in measurable terms.* Do not forget this rule. Writing a measurable goal could cause your grant proposal to be rejected for funding.

Objectives, on the other hand, are measurable (quantifiable). They are steps or benchmarks that must be achieved in order to reach the project's goals or outcomes. A good way to check your objective's measurability is to use the S.M.A.R.T. approach. Your objectives must be s̲pecific, m̲easurable, a̲ttainable, r̲ealistic, and t̲ime-bound.

The information requested in this subsection can be written in narrative form or presented in a four-column table. Figure 6.1 on page 66 presents an example of how to structure this section in narrative format. Note that the timelines are built into the objectives in this example.

Presenting this subsection in a table actually gives the grant reviewer a better overview of your project. The table on page 67 illustrates how to fill in a modified version of the United Way of America's logic model. This model, *Measuring Program Outcomes—A Practical Approach,* is widely accepted by grantmakers and is available from several sources, including online.

When you use this format, you must align each column across so that your inputs, goals, objectives, and outcomes follow a logical implementation sequence. Also when you use this format, you must include a separate timeline chart, such as the one on page 68, where you list your key program activities and show the start date for each activity. Some funders will require a project start date. In this NNG Common Grant Application Format, the start date appears on the Cover Sheet behind *Period Grant Will Cover.* For example: June 20, 2004 to June 19, 2005. However, in the timeline chart, I tend to put activities in quarters. Project start dates can be delayed, so I prefer to generalize in this table.

Figure 6.1

Sample Narrative Format

Goal 1: Provide parents with the skills they need to find and keep a job that helps keep their family intact.

Objective 1a: At the end of the fourth quarter, a minimum of 50% of the Even Start parent participants will demonstrate a growth/change in one or more areas of basic skills in reading, mathematics, or language by a minimum of 1.0 grade level, as evidenced by pre- and post-test scores on the TABE (Test for Adult Basic Education).

Objective 1b: By the end of the second quarter, a minimum of 65% of parent participants who have identified a high school diploma as their goal and who have been enrolled at least 18 weeks in Even Start will earn credit toward a diploma.

Implementation activities: After observing the parents' communication abilities, the Home Visitor will verbally administer a quick literacy assessment questionnaire to ascertain the level of education attained by each parent. Once it is established that one or more of the parents lacks a GED or high school diploma and/or basic reading skills, the parent(s) will be referred to their local Adult Basic Education (ABE) program (at one of the county's LEAs—local education agencies—or Southwestern Missouri College). The Adult Basic Education site will administer pre-test assessments using a six-interval skill scale in order to place the parent at the appropriate "educational functioning level" at the start of an instructional period. Post-test assessments will indicate advancements on this scale. Parents will be assessed using one or more of eight standard ABE/ESL proficiency tests, depending on which is the most prescriptive assessment for their Family Action Plan outcome goals.

Table 3

Program Logic Model

Inputs	Goals	Measurable Objectives	Outcomes
The resources needed to operate the grant-funded program	*What the program does to fulfill its mission*	*The direct products of program activities*	*Benefits for participants during and after the program funding period*
• Money • Staff and staff time • Volunteers and volunteer time • Facilities • Equipment • Supplies	• Provide • Educate • Counsel • Create • Conduct	• Number of classes taught • Number of sessions conducted • Number of educational materials distributed • Number of hours of service delivered • Number of participants served	• Gained new knowledge • Increased skills • Changed attitudes or values • Modified behavior • Improved conditions • Altered status

Table 4

Implementation Timeline

Key Activities	Start Timeline			
Quarters	1st	2nd	3rd	4th
Activity 1	◉			
Activity 2		◉		

Recommended length. The subsection should begin on the bottom of page 3, fill all of page 4, and if needed, take up the top half of page 5. You are nearly done with Section B.

Visual enhancements. Add 10% gray shading to the first row of your tables. If one of your tables carries over to a second or third page, remember to copy and paste the header row at the top of the table where it starts on each new page. With the columns labeled, it will be unnecessary for the reviewer to flip back and forth between pages to see what each column discusses.

4. Statement of how the project proposes to serve all groups equally regardless of race, class, gender, ethnicity, age, or sexual orientation, and how it will accommodate individuals with physical disabilities or language barriers

Primer. In this subsection give the grant reviewer your school's or district's assurances for open access and fair treatment for all. You can respond to this subsection in one all-encompassing sentence or with a small narrative that addresses each group individually. Watch your space constraints; you still have one more narrative subsection to include.

Recommended length. One sentence or one short paragraph. You will likely be typing on page 5 of the Common Grant Application narrative.

Visual enhancements. Use no graphics in this subsection.

5. Description of the systemic or social change the school or district is trying to achieve

Primer. In this subsection summarize for the grant reviewer your vision of how your grant-funded activities will address and change the underlying or root causes of the problem presented in the Problem Statement. Your description should reference which models your project will use.

Figure 6.2 (page 70) is an example of how to structure and word your response to this subsection.

Recommended length. Use the remainder of page 5. Do not type beyond page 5. If your grant goes onto a sixth page, you may reduce the font size in your tables to 11 point to help shorten the narrative to five pages.

Visual enhancements. Use no graphics in this subsection.

(continued on page 71)

Figure 6.2

Sample Change Description

Five-Year Social Change Initiative

The Hillside County Even Start Family Literacy Program will put into place a five-year social change initiative that will eliminate the problems associated with adult illiteracy and parenting skills deficiencies. Envisioned long-term outcomes include:

- Parents will be trained to interact with their child. (The Kenan and Even Start Home Visitation model will be implemented countywide.)

- Parents will be introduced to early childhood resources at local libraries and will receive transportation assistance that enables them to attend meetings with other parents and participate in child-parent interactive literacy events (Kenan).

- Parents will be connected to the community and will have access to adult education services and programs. (The Equipped for the Future model will be implemented countywide.)

- Parents will receive the skilled training needed to find and keep a job that helps keep their family intact (Kenan and Equipped for the Future).

- Parents will understand the power and influence they have over their children and what causes academic failure (Kenan and Even Start Home Visitation).

- Parents will be shown how to create a family climate for celebrating gains in their child's developmental progress (Kenan and Even Start Home Visitation).

With your grant funding support, Hillside County parents will be equipped and empowered to care for their children and families in the future.

III. ATTACHMENTS

A. Evaluation

Brief description of your plan for evaluating the success of the project

Primer. In this first attachment section, lay out the plan for evaluating attainment of the project's measurable objectives. You will tell the reviewer what questions will be addressed, who will be involved in evaluating the work (staff, parents, community members, consultants), and how the evaluation results will be used. You should also indicate that the evaluation would be qualitative (includes feedback on quality of services and training), quantitative (includes measures, such as head counts), formative (includes frequent data collection, interpretation, and reporting), and summative (includes a comprehensive end of funding evaluation report). The W. K. Kellogg Foundation has developed an *Evaluation Handbook*. The Web site link is http://www.wkkf.org/Pubs/Tools/Evaluation/Pub770.pdf. This is a popular reference for grant writers and has a great set of evaluation tutorials.

Recommended length. Do not exceed three pages of single-spaced text with double spacing between paragraphs.

Visual enhancements. Since the attachments are three to four times larger than the Common Grant Application narrative, include section cover sheets to help orient the grant reviewer. Before each evaluation section, insert a cover sheet with the section title (for example, "Attachment A. Evaluation") in boldface, 24-point type centered on the page. These dividers organize what otherwise might be a stack of 10 to 20 pages of supporting documentation.

B. Organizational Structure/Administration

Note: For the following attachments, keep the page length to a minimum. Whenever possible, consolidate two pages of information into one page by lowering the point size or making reduced copies. This means reducing lengthy documents by 50% and printing two document pages on one 8½ x 11 size sheet of paper.

1. Brief description of how your school or district works: What are the responsibilities of the board, staff, and volunteers?

Primer. In this subsection provide an overview of the management plan for the district or school.

2. Identify who will be involved in carrying out the plans outlined in the grant request

Primer. In this subsection introduce the key personnel or management team for the grant-funded project. Do not include full biographies, résumés, or curriculum vitae.

3. List your board of education members with related demographic information

Primer. In this subsection the grant reviewer is looking for board member names, addresses, occupations, board titles, terms of service (beginning and ending dates), gender, and ethnicity. Funding agencies often favor schools and organizations whose board members reflect the demographics of the community, including the target population you propose to serve.

4. Description of the board selection process: How is the board selected, who selects members, and how often?

Primer. This subsection usually refers to 501(c)(3) non-profit organizations, not schools. However, just to make sure you have responded to all areas of concern, at the end of your board of education list include some language from the bylaws about nominations, protocol for board member appointment or election, and term limits.

5. Organizational chart showing your decision-making structure

Primer. In this last subsection of Part B of the attachments, the grant reviewer wants to see a one-page organizational chart that illustrates the line of authority from the project personnel level to the administrator responsible for project management oversight.

C. Finances

Note: For the following attachments, keep the page length to a minimum. Whenever possible, consolidate two pages of information into one page by lowering the point size or making reduced copies. This means reducing lengthy documents by 50% and printing two document pages on one 8½ x 11 size sheet of paper.

1. Most recent full-year district financial statement—audited, if available

Primer. For this attachment the grant reviewer wants to see a combined financial statement (expenses, revenue, and balance sheet), preferably audited. Do not attach a cumbersome spiral-bound financial report. Instead, have your financial officer or business manager pull out the sections that show the combined budget for the general fund.

2. District's current annual operating budget and projected operating budget for upcoming year

Primer. Work with your financial officer or business manager to condense the data in these two budgets so it fits into a spreadsheet that prints out in landscape view on one or two standard-sized sheets of paper.

3. Current project budget

Primer. The NNG Common Grant Application format comes with a recommended budget format. If you already prepare project budgets that fit this format, you can submit them in their original forms. You may also reproduce the budget format shown on the following pages on your computer and/or submit separate pages for income and expenses.

4. Description of your plans for future fundraising

Primer. In this subsection the grant reviewer is really asking you to discuss sustainability. How will you continue to provide the services to your target population after the grant funds have been spent? Work with your financial officer or

(continued on page 77)

BUDGET

EXPENSES	
Item	**Amount**
Salaries [break down by individual position and indicate full-time equivalent (FTE)]	$
Fringe benefits and payroll taxes	
Consultants and professional fees	
Travel	
Equipment	
Supplies	
Training	
Printing and copying	
Telephone and fax	
Postage and delivery	
Rent and utilities	
In-kind expenses	
Other [specify in detail]	
TOTAL EXPENSES	**$**

(continued)

BUDGET (continued)

INCOME	
Source	**Amount**
Government grants and contracts [name the funding agency and give the amount of each grant or contract committed to the grant proposal project]	$
Foundations [name the foundations and give the amounts of all grants pending for the grant proposal project]	
Corporations [list the corporations and give the total amount each committed for the grant proposal project]	
United Way [some schools qualify for United Way grants]	
Individual contributions [list the total committed without names]	
Fundraising events and products	
In-kind support [give details of sources and amounts; be sure to calculate the value of your volunteers' time]	
Other [earned program income, consulting fees, and so on; specify sources and amounts]	
TOTAL INCOME	$
BALANCE [subtract **total** expenses from **total** income]*	$

*This balance should come out to zero. All of your known and proposed income line items should offset the total project expenses.

business manager to draft a statement that your school will be able to continue the project at some level.

D. Other Supporting Material

Note: In this subsection, make a final pitch for your project by showing why your school or district is deserving of support. Do not send videos, audiocassettes, or CD-ROMs to funders. Do send:

1. Letters of support/commitment (up to three)

2. Recent newsletter articles, newspaper clippings, evaluations, or reviews (up to three)

3. Recent district report card (retrieve it from your state department of education Web site if your business office does not have a copy)

4. Other supporting documentation (problem statement research and other relevant information)

CHECK THE RULES AGAIN

Now that you have finished writing your grant, take a few minutes to quickly review the funding source's guidelines to make sure nothing was overlooked and to determine how many copies of the grant proposal you need to send. Though the guidelines will not tell you this, if you are submitting a grant proposal for a project related to environmental education, use recycled paper for all the pages in the grant proposal package and use a recycled paper catalog-size envelope.

GOOD NEWS FROM THE FAIRY GODMOTHER

It can take up to 18 months after you mail your grant proposal to be notified of a funding award from a foundation. If the foundation plans to fund your grant proposal, you will be notified by letter or e-mail. Some foundations will require that your school or district sign a grant award agreement before they issue the award check. But most foundations are like fairy godmothers—that is, they issue your entire grant award in one check, up front, and usually with no strings attached. It is up to the school or district to generate frequent evaluation and expense reports back to their new funding partner.

CHALK IT UP TO EXPERIENCE

Regretfully, not all grant proposals sent to foundations are funded. Usually your school or district contact person will receive notification of rejection within 6 months of the date you mailed the proposal. The rejection form letter will not provide much detail on why your proposal was rejected for funding consideration. Only rarely will you receive written review comments on your proposal from a foundation. Often, however, a telephone call to the contact person on the rejection notice and a request for verbal comments will result in your school or district being invited to submit a revised proposal in the next funding cycle. Taking the funder's advice, you may very well convert a loss into a win—if not with that funder, then with other funders you approach.

ACTION STEPS

Gather needed information. Whether you work alone or with a grant writing team, gather the information you need to write each section of the grant proposal narrative before you begin writing. With this information in hand, you will be able to maintain momentum and interest in your task once you start writing and will not have to stop writing until you have at least completed the narrative.

Organize information. You can eliminate uncertainty about what information you have and where it goes in the narrative by collating it in file folders labeled for each narrative subsection. Drop in the folders any documents, notes, charts, and other items that you plan to use for each subsection. Place the folders in a vertical file in the same order as they appear in the narrative.

Check for readability. If more than one person writes the sections of the narrative, make sure to assign someone other than the contributing writers to read the proposal for consistency in terms, style, and formatting.

Chapter 7

Exploring State Department of Education Grant Applications

As an educator, most of your grant writing projects will be related to your district, school, or classroom needs. Once you have mastered corporate and foundation grant proposals, the logical progression is to begin exploring your state department of education's competitive grant funding opportunities. This chapter focuses on the technical aspects of state-level grant applications.

YOUR FIRST STATE DEPARTMENT OF EDUCATION GRANT APPLICATION

You just received your first state department of education grant application. There are 30 or more pages of instructions. Where do you start? Begin by looking at the basic components and requirements of all state-level education grant applications.

Introduction and background. This section of the grant application provides information on the federal legislative act that led to the grant funding opportunity. Your state department of education has either received a significantly large formula grant allocation or it has applied for and received a competitive grant award from the U.S. Department of Education. Federal grants awarded through a state agency are referred to as *pass-through* funding. This section also tells you what types of activities the act is authorized to fund. Pay attention to any wording in **boldface.** When the state agency boldfaces or italicizes a phrase or sentence, this indicates the material is of critical importance. Most importantly, this section tells you your state's funding allocation, or the amount of money available for regranting through the competitive grant application process. Regranting means to "grant again." The process is as follows: Congress allocates funds to federal agencies. Federal agencies keep some of the money for administrative expenses, and either through a formula allocation or competitive grantmaking, Congress passes these monies through (pass-through) to State Education Agencies (SEAs). In turn, the SEAs keep a portion of the federal monies for administrative expenses. The remaining monies are regranted through either formula allocations or competitive grantmaking to Local Education Agencies (LEAs), also known as school districts.

Program description. This section describes the purpose of the grant and expands upon the federal legislative act's authorized activities. It also states the types of educational agencies that can apply for the earmarked competitive grant funds. Some grant competitions are open only to LEAs. Others are open to other types of educational divisions, such as higher education institutions, education associations, and community-wide partnerships where an LEA is the lead partner and grant applicant for a consortium.

Key features of the authorizing activities. This section contains an extensive list of authorized activities. Read through the list twice. On the first pass highlight the activities that fall within your school improvement plan. On the second pass underline the specific activities that your school or district has the capacity to undertake—if funded—during the next school year. Most state education agency grants are awarded on 1-year cycles. Some are renewable, but most are not.

The authorizing act is usually very general, allowing states to specify the relevant types of programs they will fund. This section also stipulates your state's priorities for funding under the act and gives the number of grants your state intends to award and the range of grant funding.

Proposal requirements. This section specifies the layout for the narrative section of the grant proposal. It will specify mandatory line spacing (double or single); minimum font size (usually a 12-point font); page limitations (*"shall not exceed . . ."*); and margin settings (minimum 1 inch). You must adhere to these formatting requirements. Being out of compliance can result in your grant application being eliminated during the technical review process and never being read.

Standard forms. Your state education agency grant application package will have these standard forms: cover page, assurances, and partner sign-off. All of the forms have easily understood instructions. Your financial officer or business manager can provide your school's or district's state-assigned school identification number, which you will need to enter on the forms. Because your superintendent or other authorized person will need to sign all forms, it is a good idea to get his or her signature in advance. You do not want to do this last because you could miss the deadline if your superintendent is unavailable to sign the forms when the time comes to mail in the application. Most government agencies will not accept rubber stamp signatures. They want the original John Hancock.

State education agency grant applications are my favorite to write. Why? They get right to the point. You know what they want and when they want it. Most state education agencies limit their narrative writing requirements to 10 pages, maximum—unlike the 25 to 40 pages required in a federal grant application narrative. Your chances of getting funded are a lot higher at the state level, as well.

Another positive point of the state grant is that there is no hidden agenda like there can be in federal funding agencies. When I say hidden agenda, I mean that some federal agencies that award grant monies write the grant guidelines based on legislative requirements and agency protocol. However, often there are hidden agendas when it comes to who will actually win a coveted grant award. The following chapter will describe in detail how to avoid being a victim of such hidden agendas (pages 105–107).

Abstract. Some state education agency grant applications include a template for the abstract and allow the grant applicant to recreate the form with a computer using word processing. Although the abstract will be near the beginning of your final grant application package (under the cover form, assurances, and partner-sign-off pages), you should write the abstract last because it is so important. This one-page summary, usually of 200 words or less, should increase the reviewer's interest by providing a glimpse at some of the key concepts in the full grant application narrative. In addition, the state education agency uses the one-page summary to announce your grant award to the public in print and online. An expeditious way to create the abstract narrative is to copy key sentences from each narrative section of the completed grant application and paste them into the abstract. Make sure this new section reads well on its own.

Rubrics rule! Most state education agency grant applications provide tiered review criteria rubrics for each section of the grant application narrative. These rubrics range from Not Recommended for Funding (0–1 review points) to Recommended for Funding with Revisions (2–6 review points) to Recommended for Funding (7–10 review points). While most grant competitions top out at 100 maximum review points, others may have 140, 180, or even 240 total review points. The total review points do not really matter. What does matter is that you write each grant application section so your competitive narrative response is placed in the Recommended for Funding rubric's point range.

Table 7.1 (page 86) shows a sample rating rubric used by grant reviewers to score the abstract section.

Write to meet all the standards. The instructions in the guidelines and the review criteria for the same application narrative section are not always mutually inclusive. For example, an actual grant application kit issued by a state education agency gave these instructions for writing an abstract: "Provide a one-page summary (200 words) that briefly describes the project vision, goals, activities, and key features that will be addressed and expected benefits of work." However, the same grant application kit's Recommended for Funding rubric stated: "The abstract contains all elements required on one page (description of collaboration, the project,

Table 7.1

Sample Abstract Rating Rubric

Not Recommended for Funding	Recommended for Funding With Revisions	Recommended for Funding
The abstract is missing.	The abstract minimally describes the initiative; portions of the required elements are missing or are labeled "see attached."	The abstract contains all elements required on one page (description of collaboration, the project, research base, project evaluation and outcomes, and applicant's commitment).

research base, project evaluation and outcomes, and applicant's commitment)." If you followed the proposal requirements guidelines for the abstract, you would be missing descriptions of your collaboration, the research base, and perhaps even the project evaluation language and your school's or district's commitment. This would cause you to lose points.

When the state brings in peer reviewers to work in teams to read and score grant applications, they use only the review criteria to judge them. There are no exceptions. So forget the narrative instructions—study the review criteria and write responses that will get each section the highest rubric ratings.

ELEMENTS OF THE PROGRAM NARRATIVE

The elements or sections typically contained in a project narrative for state education agency grant applications are listed below, followed by a discussion of what you need to do to completely answer each section to satisfy the needs of the grantmaker.

Demonstration of need. Develop a problem statement based on your understanding and research findings of your school's or district's needs. These needs should be correlated with your state's curriculum framework standards for the targeted area of academic improvement. You will want to include data related to student achievement. For example, if educators at your school need additional staff development training in the core content areas, you should describe teaching application deficiencies in this section.

Research or evidence base. Discuss and cite the current research or evidence relevant to the proposed project. The literature you cite should clearly indicate why the proposed activities were selected or designed. If this proposal builds on prior work, the project narrative should indicate what was learned from that work and how the lessons learned are incorporated in the project.

Plan of work. Clearly describe the goals and objectives for the project and the responsibility of each of the partners (all funders expect you to have community partners). Your plan of work must include a timeline and an estimate of the number, type, duration, and intensity of all proposed activities. This is the section where you will make a compelling case for the activities of the project and describe how the activities will help your state education agency build rigorous, cumulative, reproducible, and usable evidence-based research. Any proposed professional development activities must be integrated with your school improvement goals.

In addition, you must show the grant reviewer how all of the project activities align with the state's content and professional development standards.

Management capability. Clearly demonstrate that your school or district is capable of exhibiting expertise in the content area, managing the project, organizing the work, and meeting deadlines.

Sustainability. In this section, you must present evidence that your state grant-funded project can be sustained beyond the life of the grant funding.

Evaluation plan. Most government grants, including those from state education agencies, require that the evaluator be an independent contractor. In this section, you will describe how your school or district will contract with an independent evaluator to design, collect, and analyze data about the project model, curriculum, and impact on both participating and control students and teachers. Most state agencies will expect your school or district to participate in the state-level evaluation of the federally funded grant program. The evaluation plan will contain information that you already provided to grant reviewers in the plan of work. You should not refer the grant reviewer back to the plan of work. Instead, you will need to create tables that present, in clear and concise language, your measurable objectives and the monthly, quarterly, or annual progress targets. In addition, you will include a statement about how you plan to collect the data and report your results to the state education agency.

Budget summary and detail. You will most likely be using state education agency forms for your budget summary. However, you will have to develop a detailed budget narrative. Work closely with your financial officer or business manager to determine *future* expenses for each line item on the state budget forms. Remember, budget items must be clearly tied to the scope and requirements of the proposed grant-funded project. You must include in the budget a provision for an independent evaluator, funds for key staff to participate in any state-level technical assistance meetings, and a description of all matching or in-kind contributions of your school or district and from your partners.

Appendix or attachments. Grant reviewers are only expected to read and score the abstract and the body of the program narrative. However, most state education agencies ask for specific attachments. These may include:

- Letters of commitment from the partners

- Résumés of key faculty and staff

- Elaboration of data used to establish the need

- Evidence of impact from prior grant-funded efforts

- Elaboration of research or evidence used to design the proposed project model

BE ATTENTIVE TO DETAIL

Before you mail the final grant application package, read the grant application submission instructions again to verify the grant competition's closing date, delivery address, and number of copies needed in addition to the original document. You can track when the package is delivered if you purchase a U.S. Postal Service Delivery Confirmation receipt when you mail it.

LESSONS LEARNED

I once wrote a state department of education grant for a country school district. The proposal was for a paid teacher sabbatical program. I neglected to pay attention to the value and accuracy of my software's spell checker. I must have used the word "sabbatical" at least 22 times, and each time the spell checker highlighted the word for correction, I skipped over the recommendation. I thought the word "sabbatical" was not in the program's dictionary, and assumed I had spelled the word correctly.

The grant draft went to the school superintendent and he gave his approval, with no changes. I finalized the narrative and packaged the grant application for district signatories and forwarding to the department of education.

Some months later the award letter arrived from the state superintendent of education. It congratulated my client, the district, on winning a grant award for the "sabbitical" project. "Sabbatical" was incorrectly spelled "sabbitical" throughout the grant application. My client, however, did receive a record award. The mistake was realized the minute we read the award letter. I learned my lesson about spell check and software dictionaries! It was shortly after this embarrassing moment that I decided to retain the services of a proofreading/editing company.

THE APPLICATION IS IN THE MAIL

Once you send your grant application package to the state education agency, what happens on their end? After the grant application deadline has passed, department staff review the proposals received for completeness and compliance with the requirements of the act to determine applicant eligibility. The staff will reject any grant applications that are received late (after the deadline), are significantly incomplete, or have an ineligible applicant agency.

Expert review panel. The grant applications that pass technical review are given to an expert review panel. The panel evaluates eligible applications based on the required application components and the established criteria defined in the scoring rubrics. After reviewing all the applications, the review panel makes recommendations for funding to the state education agency.

FINAL DISCUSSIONS PRIOR TO YOUR AWARD

Following the review, the state education agency may contact you to discuss any modifications to the project plan that may be required. In addition, in order to maximize the effects of limited funds, applicants whose grants are recommended at less than the amount of grant funds requested may be asked to revise their project budgets and plans of work.

IF YOU RECEIVE A REJECTION LETTER

If you receive a rejection letter from your state education agency, call or write the person who notified you and request a copy of the expert review panel's written comments on the strengths and weaknesses of your grant application. You should be able to receive a copy of the review results without having to cite the Freedom of Information Act (FOIA) language in your request. If you do need a sample of the FOIA, take a look at the Web site belonging to the Freedom of Information Center at the Missouri School of Journalism: http://foi.missouri.edu/foialett.html. You will need to modify some of the language to fit your specific information request.

Retool your grant application. Not all is lost if your application is rejected. Rejected state education agency grant applications may be rewritten and resubmitted for funding consideration in the state's next funding cycle. If you clearly understand which areas of your application the expert peer reviewers indicated as weak, you will be able to improve them to earn more review points when a revised application is submitted later.

Get on the inside track. Volunteer to be an expert review panel member before the next funding cycle begins. This experience will give you insight into how the agency thinks and what the state really wants to fund. Your knowledge will help you avoid rejection letters. First, contact your SEA to see if they have opportunities for peer review. Second, check with the U.S. Department of Education's Web site for "Call for Peer Reviewers" announcements. The URL is www.ed.gov. Type "peer reviewers" in the SearchEd.gov box and note that peer reviewers are also called Field Readers, so try searching for announcements with both terms.

Look for other funders. In addition to submitting a revised application during the next funding cycle, you can bring together your grant writing team to find alternative corporate and foundation funding sources likely to be interested in funding all or some components of your project. Never, ever give up. Failures can only become successes when we refuse to accept them.

ACTION STEPS

Act quickly. Ask your superintendent to reroute any state education agency grant opportunity announcements to you immediately. You want to have as much time as possible to plan, research, and write your winning grant application.

Mark up the guidelines. Highlight and tab all key sections. Note any special signatory requirements, particularly on the application forms, and take care of them as soon as possible. Compile a list of questions you have about the application and call the contact for clarification.

Attend technical assistance meetings. State education agencies often hold pre-application technical assistance conferences. If you can, attend these conferences, take notes, and ask questions. Sometimes the information exchanged at these meetings is different than the information in the application guidelines. Attending the meeting could make the difference in your grant application being funded or rejected.

Chapter 8

The Big Kahuna:
Federal Department of Education
Grant Applications

WHEN YOU PROGRESS TO THIS LEVEL OF GRANT WRITING, you are entering into the world of nationwide competition. What does it take to win a coveted federal grant award? Can anyone write a federal grant application and have a fair chance in the competition? What do you really need to know in order to consistently win federal grant awards? Because every level of grant writing is more detailed than the level before, your progression from letter proposals to foundation grants to state education agency grant applications has given you the background and knowledge to prepare federal Department of Education grant applications. Can you start your grant writing endeavors at the federal level? Yes, if you have a knack for research, details, and filtering through technical terms in order to uncover what you need to write and win a federal grant application.

WAITING FOR THE E-MAIL ALERT

Here's an insider secret: Sign up to have e-mail alerts for federal grant announcements sent directly to your inbox. You can get on the e-mail list by logging onto www.fedgrants.gov and clicking on the "Applicant" button. At the top of the next window, select "Applicant Notification Service." There you can sign up to receive alerts from the Federal Grants Opportunities (FGO) office via e-mail. After subscribing you will receive announcements of new grants and modifications to existing grant announcements. Four free subscription options are available. You can:

1. Register to receive all notices or selected notices based on funding opportunity number.

2. Register to receive all notices from selected agencies and categories of funding activities.

3. Register to receive all notices from selected interest and eligibility groups.

4. Register to receive all grants notices.

You can choose to receive only U.S. Department of Education notices, or you can select notifications from other federal agencies as well.

FINDING ANNOUNCEMENT DETAILS

One day you will check your e-mail and there will be an alert announcing a grant funding opportunity that could fund some aspect of your school's or district's school improvement vision. The e-mail will contain a link to the federal funding agency's grant announcement Web site. At the site, you can read an overview of the grant funding program and download the full application kit.

HANDLING ELECTRONIC SUBMISSIONS

Do not be surprised if the federal agency sponsoring the funding opportunity will accept *only* electronic (online) applications. This requirement is the norm for one out of three grant announcements, including those from the U.S. Department of Education. Do not fret if it is an online application—you will still plan, research, and write the complete narrative offline. When you have finished, you will simply copy pertinent portions of the narrative from your word processing program and paste them while online into the fields of the corresponding grant application narrative sections, editing as necessary. Most of the federal agencies are using standardized electronic grants management software that enables you to paste and save whole sections of an application, then log off and return later to continue entering text online.

DECIPHERING THE GRANT ANNOUNCEMENT

The packet of instructions accompanying a federal grant announcement can be 40 pages or longer, so be sure you have plenty of paper in your printer. The individual elements of the grant application kit are outlined in the following section with a brief discussion of each part and the things you should watch for as you read.

Application kit cover page. The first page on all federal grant application kits, the cover page, gives you the name of the federal agency and the specific division releasing the grant announcement. Also included on the cover page are the fiscal year for grant awards and the Catalog of Federal Domestic Assistance number

(CFDA). Highlight the CFDA number because you will need it later for your grant application cover page. Take careful note that the deadline for the grant application appears near the bottom of the cover page.

Table of contents. The table of contents lists all of the sections, including appendices, you will find in the grant application kit. Make a quick check of all sections. If you are missing forms or instructions, try downloading another copy. If you still have missing sections, call the agency and ask them to mail you a hard copy of the application kit. (The agency's contact number will be in the first five pages.)

Application notice. The application kit will include a complete copy of the *Federal Register* notice for this particular grant funding opportunity. The *Federal Register* notice is the application's most critical section. Here you will find the actual formatting and writing instructions for the grant application. A brief overview of the narrative section requirements for federal grants begins on page 102.

Program statute. This section contains the full language of the authorizing act—the legislation written and approved by Congress—that resulted in a federal funding allocation and implementation for the particular grant you are applying for. Take the act out of the application kit and set it aside to refer to later when you are planning content and researching information for the Need Statement and Project Design.

Application checklist. Yes, the federal government actually gives you a checklist to make sure you have all of the forms and sections in order in your final grant application package. The checklist also tells you how many application copies are needed by the funding agency and reminds you to get original signatures and dates on all forms. Most importantly, the checklist reminds you that you need to submit a copy of your completed grant application to the state's single point of contact (SPOC). The SPOC will be covered on the next page.

Application cover sheet. The first form in the application kit will be the Application for Federal Assistance. This document requires identifying information for the grant applicant—your school or district. It also requires that you identify the grant competition you are applying for by name and by CFDA number. *Note*: All federal grant applicants must have a D-U-N-S® number (Data Universal Numbering System; also referred to as DUNS). This unique, nine-digit number does not convey any identifying information about the grant applicant and is used by federal agencies for grant award tracking purposes. A set of explicit instructions for each entry field accompanies the form. Your school district can obtain a D-U-N-S number at no charge by registering online at http://www.grants.gov/RequestaDUNS.

Budget forms. The budget summary form comprises two pages: Section A (Summary of U.S. Department of Education Funds) and Section B (Summary of Non-Federal Funds). Depending on the federal grant competition, there may or may not be instructions for these two forms. However, your financial officer or business manager will understand the line items and be able to help you and your grant writing team use information from the detailed budget narrative to fill in the forms.

Assurances. All government grants require that grant applicants sign and date a series of assurances related to receiving federal funding awards. To the signatory of these documents (usually the school superintendent) the language must seem intimidating. However, it is extremely important that the forms be signed and dated or your grant application will not pass the technical review process.

Certifications. Your superintendent or authorized signatory will also be required to sign statements, or certifications, guaranteeing a drug-free workplace and addressing lobbying, debarment, suspension, and other matters of responsibility.

General Education Provisions Act. This enclosure informs you about a provision in the Department of Education's General Education Provisions Act (GEPA), Section 427, that applies to applicants for new grant awards under department programs. *All grant applicants must include information in their grant application narrative addressing this provision in order to receive federal funding.* What does GEPA boil down to? That your school or district ensures equitable access to, and participation in, their federally assisted program for students, teachers, and other program beneficiaries with special needs.

Intergovernmental review of federal programs. Executive Order 12372 requires you to send an extra copy of your federal grant application to a single point of contact in your state. In some states, this will be a state-level clearinghouse and in other states the SPOC will be an agency or individual designated by the governor (only a few states do not have SPOCs). Every grant application kit comes with a list of the SPOCs. You can also find the most up-to-date list of SPOCs at the Office of Management and Budget Web site (http://www.whitehouse.gov/omb/grants/spoc.html). You must mail the SPOC a copy of the application the same day you mail your application package to the federal grant agency.

Application transmittal instructions. Tape or tack this page on the wall by your desk because it gives you the U.S. Postal Service mailing address and the address for delivery of the package in person or by courier service. The Application Control Center for each federal agency accepts deliveries only on weekdays (excluding federal holidays). As long as your application package is postmarked prior to the grant competition's closing date, it will be accepted for consideration. *Remember to read the grant application guidelines on each specific competition's mailing requirements for meeting the deadline.*

Selection criteria. This section is your working guide as you plan, research, and write the grant application. It tells you the selection criteria and factors that will be used by the U.S. Department of Education to evaluate grant applications. The maximum score for all of the selection criteria is usually 100 points. Remember, your application may accumulate a higher score with priority points.

DOING A QUICK SCAN

The next step is to quickly scan the Application Notice for the following critical information:

- Purpose of the program

- Eligible applicants

- Deadline for transmittal of applications

- Notification of intent to apply for funding requirements (directs you to mail or fax a letter to the federal agency notifying the agency that your school or district intends to apply for this specific funding)

- Estimated available funds

- Estimated range of awards

- Estimated average size of award

- Estimated number of awards

- Project period (states whether projects will be funded for 12 months or multiple years)

- Priority (contains language that the Secretary of Education wants to see in the application when the agency determines whether to award extra review points)

Now using the checklist (table 4.1) provided in chapter 4 (see page 36), check off "yes" or "no" to the preplanning questions and decide if all of this work is worth your time.

BLITZING THE NARRATIVE SECTION WITH KEY WORDS

You must use buzzwords that appear in the selection criteria of the U.S. Department of Education grant application. Using these words in your writing demonstrates your project's alignment with the competition's act, purpose, and priorities. The following is a list of selection criteria and some of the buzzwords you would use to show that your grant meets the criteria.

Need for project or need statement—focus, disadvantaged, serving, addressing, gaps, weaknesses, infrastructure, opportunities, magnitude

Quality of the project design—design, goals, objectives, outcomes, specific, measurable, target population, up-to-date knowledge from research and effective practice, exceptional approach, meeting statutory purposes, coordinated with other appropriate community, state, and federal resources

Quality of project service—likely impact, intended recipients, likelihood, improvements, achievement, rigorous academic standards

Quality of project personnel—relevant training, experience, consultants, subcontractors

Adequacy of resource—support, facilities, equipment, supplies, persons served, anticipated results and benefits

Quality of management plan—achieve the objectives, timely, timelines, milestones, accomplishing, project tasks, responsibilities, high-quality products and services

Quality of the project evaluation—objective performance measures, intended outcomes, quantitative and qualitative data, methods, performance feedback, periodic assessment, progress toward achieving intended outcomes

ATTACHING THE CURRICULUM VITAE

You will want to attach a complete curriculum vita (résumé) for each member of the project staff and job descriptions for positions yet to be filled. Also attach at least 10 letters of support. Before you start adding attachments, read the application checklist to see if there is a limit on the number of attachment pages. In addition, look for attachment pagination or tabbing requirements.

OBTAINING CONGRESSIONAL SUPPORT

It is critical that you notify your Congressional team's Washington, D.C., office that your school or district intends to apply for a federal grant. Why? There are several reasons. Once you send your Washington-based legislators a copy of your project abstract or initial draft application, they will write letters of support directly to the Secretary of Education regarding your grant request. Congressional letters, *which should not be mailed in with your grant application as attachments,* have no influence with the expert peer review panel; however, they do have influence on the Secretary of Education. Having Congressional letters of support on file can make the difference between your school or district being funded or rejected for funding. I cannot emphasize enough the importance of getting congressional support.

Another reason for involving your legislative team is that once you have mailed your application package to Washington, D.C., you can ask the team to track the grant's review process and keep you posted. They will need to know the tracking number that the Application Control Office assigns to your grant application. If you clip a self-addressed, stamped postcard to the front of your *original* grant application, the Control Office will stamp it with your tracking number and mail it back to you. Hang on to this number and write it down in several places. It is the only way to track your grant application during the lengthy review process.

RECEIVING AN ANSWER

The U.S. Department of Education can take up to 6 months to review grant applications for one competition. If your grant application is recommended for funding, your Congressional team will be notified first. Your legislators will issue a local press release and contact you with the news. Your superintendent will also receive a call or fax from the Office of Management and Budget to discuss the Department of Education's *best offer*. Sometimes, due to funding allocation cuts, your school or district will be offered an award that is less than the amount requested. This process is called *negotiation*. If you agree to accept less money, ask if you can resubmit your proposal with a scaled-down project design.

STARTING THE PROJECT

Once the federal red tape is out of the way, the monies will be transferred electronically on a quarterly basis.

HANDLING REJECTION

If your grant application is not recommended for federal funding, your school or district will receive a rejection letter from the U.S. Secretary of Education. You can then request a copy of the expert review panel's written critique of your grant application. You have the same options for retooling this failed application as were outlined at the end of chapter 7 (see page 92) for failed state education agency grant applications.

GETTING THINGS DONE WITH INSIDER KNOWLEDGE

As mentioned in the previous chapter, there can sometimes be hidden agendas in federal grant funding. Federal agencies that award grant monies write the grant guidelines based on legislative requirements and agency protocol; however, there can be hidden agendas when it comes to who will actually win an award. The unspoken, but widely known hidden agenda areas include:

- Earmarking grant monies for specific Congressional areas, but not publishing or talking about this occurrence.

- Publishing review criteria that does not include the "read between the lines" language about what the agency program staff really want to see funded.

How can you avoid being a victim of such hidden agendas?

1. Attend the agency's technical assistance conference. These are offered online via a Web cast and in regions around the country. There are 10 federal regions. You can find your region by contacting the Congressional representative's office for your state.

2. Sign up to be a peer reviewer at least one year before you plan to write a grant application for the specific agency. One peer review experience is worth at least one funded grant application from your school district. The peer review process reveals hidden agendas and more!

If you are having problems getting your grant applications recommended for federal funding, serving as a peer reviewer is one way to gain an advantage. Early in my grant writing career, I signed up with the U.S. Department of Education to serve as an expert peer reviewer. I reviewed applications several times on-site in Washington, D.C., and several times in my home office. The department would overnight express mail a box of applications to me for review. This experience gave me *insider knowledge*. I went from writing 1 out of 10 winning federal grant applications to writing 9 out of 10 winning federal grant applications.

Getting on an expert review panel takes a little initiative. You will have to go online and look for e-mail addresses or telephone numbers for contacts in each division of the U.S. Department of Education. When you communicate with the contacts, ask how you can sign up for an expert review panel.

Serving on a review panel takes the fear out of writing federal grant applications. You will learn what information belongs in each section and how it should be phrased. Being a reviewer also gives you a look at what federal program staffs *really* want to fund in a specific competition. You will gain an understanding of how to tweak your grant application to garner the most review points, and you will also get to read many diverse grant applications—some good, some bad, and some just plain unbelievable!

(continued)

ACTION STEPS

Just do it! Overcome your fear of lengthy and technical grant applications. Find a federal grant competition that fits your school's or district's vision and just do it—write a response.

Get up to speed. Bring yourself up to speed on the federal e-grants process. Eventually, all federal grant applications will have to be submitted online, so use the process now whenever it is a submission option.

Connect with legislators. Talk to your superintendent about hosting an annual legislative event in the district. This event can be a breakfast meeting each fall where your state and federal elected officials, or key members from their regional staffs, have the opportunity to visit your district and hear about your funding needs. Remember, elected officials work for you, me, and the rest of the taxpayers. Their responsibilities include helping the constituents in their districts. Legislators will look for potential funding opportunities and notify your school or district before any announcements are ever made to the general public.

Grant Writing Tips A to Z

EVERY LETTER OF THE ALPHABET CAN HELP NUDGE YOU into keeping on top of the grant writing game—just refer to the following list of tips.

A Always look for multiple types of funders to support your project.

B Be diligent in finding out why your grant requests were not funded.

C Continue to keep your community partners informed, and continue to build collaborations for future grant funding opportunities.

D Develop a tracking system to log grants that are written, pending, and funded and to keep track of future annual deadlines.

E Enlist colleagues to join your grant writing team.

F Find out how you can get on funding agency mailing lists.

G Give all grant writing team members a copy of the final grant application submitted for funding.

H Help other agencies in your community find grant funding opportunities and they, in turn, will help you.

I Implement a strong grants management system to assure clear audit trails and funder accountability.

J Justify to your superintendent why you need paid time during the school day to actively pursue grants for your school or district.

K Keep trying—even if you receive several rejection letters.

L Look for grant opportunities every day.

M Manage your time judiciously when writing a large grant request. After submitting it, give yourself a break to reenergize.

N Never, ever share a copy of your draft of a final grant request with your competition. Wait until the grant request has been submitted and the deadline has passed before you share a copy.

O Opportunities for grant funding are around you every day; aggressively start to apply for every opportunity.

P Package your grant with binder clips. Never use staples unless the instructions state that stapling is preferred.

Q Quicken the writing process by writing boilerplate school or district information and saving it on your computer for repeated use.

R Reiterate with administrators the need to stay connected to state and federal elected officials who represent your school or district.

S School Improvement Plan: Do not pursue a grant funding opportunity without first checking for alignment with the plan's goals.

T Take pride in writing grant requests and bringing new revenue into your school or district.

U Utilize technology to find news about grant opportunities.

W Willingly share this guide and your knowledge about grant writing with others.

X X-raying grant applications in Washington, D.C., is a common procedure. Postal and courier delivery trucks have to line up to have all of their packages x-rayed. Mail your federal grant applications at least 2 days before the due date to allow some lead time in case there is inclement weather or a national crisis.

Y Youth are the reason you are employed. When you have planning meetings to discuss grant opportunities, invite parents and older youth to provide stakeholder feedback.

Z Zip disks hold more data than traditional 1.44 MB floppy disks. Back up all of your grant-related files to zip disks or to a CD. Never, ever trust your hard drive to store the one copy of your in-progress grant request or boilerplate.

References and Additional Resources

ELECTRONIC RESOURCES

Annie E. Casey Foundation

http://www.aecf.org/kidscount

You will find links on the Home page to the Kids Count data. This information, available for each state on a county-by-county basis, will give you an abundance of demographics to assist with writing your statement of need.

Bev Browning & Associates

http://www.grantsconsulting.com

This Web site is home to the author of *Grant Writing for Educators*. Bev lists services for school districts and current workshop information.

Catalog of Federal Domestic Assistance

http://12.46.245.173/cfda/cfda.html

Operated by the U.S. government, the online Catalog of Federal Domestic Assistance (CFDA) gives you access to a database of all federal programs available to state and local governments (including the District of Columbia); federally-recognized Indian tribal governments; Territories (and possessions) of the United States; domestic public, quasi-public, and private profit and nonprofit organizations and institutions; specialized groups; and individuals. After you find the program you want, contact the office that administers the program and find out how to apply.

Department of Housing and Urban Development (HUD)
http://www.hud.gov/
This Web site provides links to regional U.S. Department of Housing and Urban Development offices where you can check your Colonias Zone status (if your school is located near the U.S.-Mexico border).

DOGPILE®
http://www.dogpile.com
This search engine brings together in one place results from all the leading engines—Google™, Yahoo®, Ask Jeeves®, LookSmart®, FindWhat®, and more.

Education To Go
http://www.educationtogo.com
This low-cost online training provider offers courses in the basics of proposal writing, advanced proposal writing, and becoming a grant writing consultant.

Federal Register
http://www.gpoaccess.gov/fr/index.html
Grant announcements from federal agencies are published daily in the *Federal Register.* This document can be viewed at local

libraries designated as Federal Depositories or can be found online at the U.S. Government Printing Office (GPO) Access Website (http://www.gpoaccess.gov/fr/index.html). The *Federal Register* lists all government business transactions, including grant funding or grant availability announcements.

Foundation Center
http://www.fdncenter.org
Headquartered in New York City, the Center is the premier provider of grant funding directories via print and online subscription-based access.

Foundation Center/RFP Bulletin
http://fdncenter.org/pnd/rfp/
The Foundation Center/RFP Bulletin site is the home of the Philanthropy News Digest, which lists weekly Request For Proposals (RFPs) from foundations and corporations.

Google™
http://www.google.com
The Google search engine can assist you in finding obscure grant funding opportunities for your school district. Some of the search terms to use include: grants for computers, grants for science equipment, grants for school theatrical performances, grants for arts and culture, grants for school building funds, and so forth.

The Grant Book Company/Grant Search Central
http://www.thegrantbook.com/cgi-bin/index.cgi
This Web site gives you access to federal, state, foundation, and corporate grants and programs in one easy to access online store.

Grants.gov

http://www.grants.gov

Grants.gov allows organizations to electronically find and apply for competitive grant opportunities from all federal grant making agencies. It is the single access point for over 900 grant programs offered by the 26 federal grant-making agencies. Click on the "Get Started" link to find out how to locate grant opportunities and download application packages.

GrantStation

http://www.grantstation.com

This membership Web site is used by nonprofit organizations to expand their capacity, find new sources of funding, and thereby enhance their grantseeking skills.

The Grantsmanship Center

http://www.tgci.com

TGCI offers more than 200 workshops in grantsmanship and proposal writing within the United States each year.

Harris Infosource™

http://www.harrisinfo.com

This subscription-based Web site researches and compiles business information and provides high-quality data on corporations.

Hoovers Online

http://www.hoovers.com/free/

This Web site allows you to find contact information for U.S. and international corporations. You can search by company name or industry keyword. Hoovers also has a subscription-based search service where you can obtain more detailed information.

National Network of Grantmakers

http://www.nng.org

> Do not be discouraged by the small list of member foundations listed on the downloadable template. I can assure you that most foundations will accept this format, providing they do not have their own customized application form.

Realityworks, Inc.

http://www.realityworksinc.com

> This Web site contains a wealth of information for parenting education, substance abuse prevention, and consumer education teachers. Take a look at the Funding Your Program link—it was developed by the author of this book.

Regional Association of Grantmakers

http://www.rag.org

> You will find links to each of the association's member-sites, where you will be able to download the common grant application format for your state.

School Grants

http://www.schoolgrants.com

> You will find a wealth of information on this Web site for finding school grant funding opportunities and for writing winning school grant proposals and applications. From the seemingly infinite information links to the actual examples of funded grant applications, this Web site is a winner!

Stateline.org

http://www.stateline.org

> This Web site provides politics and policy news, state by state. Use this site to find issues relating to education in your state.

Thomas Register®

http://www.thomasregister.com

Thomas Register is the most comprehensive online resource for finding companies and products manufactured in North America.

University of Massachusetts

http://www.umass.edu/research/ora/alert.html

This site lists electronic funding alert service Web sites.

University of Missouri—Columbia

Freedom of Information Center

http://foi.missouri.edu/foialett.html

This Web site gives you examples of how to word Freedom of Information Act request letters.

U.S. Department of Education

http://www.ed.gov/index.jhtml

You can view current and past grant funding opportunities, sign up for electronic grant submission, and read abstracts for previously funded grants.

U.S. Department of Justice

http://www.ncjrs.org/pdffiles/buddetws.pdf

This Web site allows you to view, save, and print a complete federal grant application budget detail worksheet in PDF format.

U.S. Office of Management and Budget

http://www.whitehouse.gov/omb/grants/spoc.html

This agency provides Single Point of Contact information for states that participate in the federal intergovernmental review process.

U.S. Office of Budget and Management

http://www.whitehouse.gov/omb/circulars/index.html

This Web site contains links to procurement and financial management circulars needed by your school's business office when managing a federal grant award.

PRINT RESOURCES

Foundation Funding

The Foundation Directory. This classic guide to America's top funders features key facts on the nation's top 10,000 foundations by total giving. This book, published annually by the Foundation Center, contains more than 399,000 descriptions of selected grants and provides fundraisers with unique insight into foundation giving priorities. You can order online at www.fdncenter.org; click on Marketplace. This book is not available in book stores.

Corporate Funding

National Directory of Corporate Giving. This comprehensive directory, published annually by the Foundation Center, features up-to-date information that helps fundraisers tap into their share of grant money earmarked by companies for nonprofit support. Since corporate philanthropic programs are closely tied to the business practices of their parent companies, fundraisers need access to as much background information as possible when shaping their grant requests. Successful corporate grantseekers research the sponsoring company, its type of business, the locations of its subsidiaries, and many other relevant facts. This book is not available in bookstores and can be ordered online at www.fdncenter.org.

Evaluation

Matheson, S. (2004). *Encyclopedia of evaluation.* Thousand Oaks, CA: Sage Publications, Inc. ISBN: 0761926097.

Preskill, H., & Russ-Eft, D. (2004). *Building evaluation capacity— 72 activities for teaching and training.* Thousand Oaks, CA: Sage Publications, Inc. ISBN: 0761928103.

Grant Management

Quick, J. A., & New, C. C. (2000). *Grant winners toolkit: Project management and evaluation.* New York: John Wiley & Sons. [Book and Disk edition]. ISBN: 0471332453.

Grant Writing

Browning, B. A. (2001). *Grant writing for dummies.* New York: John Wiley & Sons. ISBN: 0764553070.

Browning, B. A. (2000). *Fundraising with the corporate letter request.* Bev Browning & Associates. [Audio cassette] ISBN: 0967107326.

Browning, B. A. (2001). *How to become a grant writing consultant.* Bev Browning & Associates. ISBN: 0967107318.

Porter, D. (2003). *Successful school grants—Fulfilling the promise of school improvement.* D & R Publishing. ISBN: 0972727507.

About the Author

BEVERLY A. BROWNING, MPA, is a national grant writing consultant, author, presenter, and postsecondary educator. She holds a master's degree in public administration and an honorary doctorate in business administration. For nearly two decades, she has worked extensively with K–12 school districts throughout the United States to help them develop funding plans and secure more than $60 million in grant awards. Bev is a highly sought after expert in the field of grant writing. She presents over two dozen specialized grant writing workshops and has developed a 2-day grant writing academy for educators.

Bev is the author of several books, including *Grant Writing For Dummies*, *Fundraising With the Corporate Letter Request* (on audiotape), and *How to Become a Grant Writing Consultant*. Her articles have appeared in numerous professional journals and newsletters, and her 30-minute *Writing a Corporate Letter Request* tutorial on audiotape is available online at www.grantsconsulting.com.

Bev lives with her husband and cat in Buckeye, Arizona.

Make the Most of Your Professional Development Investment

Let Solution Tree schedule time for you and your staff with leading practitioners in the areas of:

- **Professional Learning Communities** with Richard DuFour, Robert Eaker, Rebecca DuFour, and associates
- **Effective Schools** with associates of Larry Lezotte
- **Assessment *for* Learning** with Rick Stiggins and associates
- **Crisis Management and Response** with Cheri Lovre
- **Discipline With Dignity** with Richard Curwin and Allen Mendler
- **SMART School Teams** with Jan O'Neill and Anne Conzemius
- **Passport to Success** (parental involvement) with Vickie Burt
- **Peacemakers** (violence prevention) with Jeremy Shapiro

Additional presentations are available in the following areas:

- At-Risk Youth Issues
- Bullying Prevention/Teasing and Harassment
- Team Building and Collaborative Teams
- Data Collection and Analysis
- Embracing Diversity
- Literacy Development
- Motivating Techniques for Staff and Students

Solution Tree
formerly national educational service

304 W. Kirkwood Avenue
Bloomington, IN 47404-5132
(812) 336-7700
(800) 733-6786 (toll-free number)
FAX (812) 336-7790
e-mail: info@solution-tree.com
www.solution-tree.com

NEED MORE COPIES OR ADDITIONAL RESOURCES ON THIS TOPIC?

Need more copies of this book? Want your own copy? Need additional resources on this topic? If so, you can order additional materials by using this form or by calling us toll free at (800) 733-6786 or (812) 336-7700. Or you can order by FAX at (812) 336-7790, or visit our website at www.solution-tree.com.

Title	Price*	Quantity	Total
Grant Writing for Educators	$ 9.95		
Creating Successful Inclusion Programs	9.95		
Building Classroom Communities	9.95		
Motivating Students Who Don't Care	9.95		
Teasing and Harassment	9.95		
Building Successful Partnerships	18.95		
EdMarketing	24.95		
Parents Assuring Student Success	24.95		
PASSport to Success	179.00		
Professional Learning Communities at Work	24.95		
	SUBTOTAL		
	SHIPPING Continental U.S.: Please add 6% of order total. Outside continental U.S.: Please add 8% of order total.		
	HANDLING Continental U.S.: Please add $4. Outside continental U.S.: Please add $6.		
	TOTAL (U.S. funds)		

*Price subject to change without notice.

❏ Check enclosed ❏ Purchase order enclosed
❏ Money order ❏ VISA, MasterCard, Discover, or American Express (circle one)

Credit Card No._____ Exp. Date_____
Cardholder Signature _____

SHIP TO:
First Name_____ Last Name _____
Position _____
Institution Name_____
Address _____
City_____ State_____ ZIP _____
Phone_____ FAX_____
E-mail _____

304 West Kirkwood Avenue
Bloomington, IN 47404-5132
(812) 336-7700 • (800) 733-6786 (toll-free number)
FAX (812) 336-7790
e-mail: orders@solution-tree.com
www.solution-tree.com

Solution Tree
formerly national educational service